Facilitation Skills

Helping
Groups
Make Decisions

Simple Steps to Help Groups & Teams
Focus on the Issue and
Build Agreement on Solutions

Gregory B. Putz

ISBN 0-9664456-0-0

First Edition, First Printing

Library of Congress Cataloging-in-Publication Data

Putz, Gregory B. (Gregory Bryan), 1952-
    Facilitation skills : helping groups make decisions / Gregory B.
Putz. -- 1st ed.
        p.   cm.
    Includes bibliographical references (p.   ) and index.
    ISBN 0-9664456-0-0 (pbk.)
    1. Teams in the workplace. 2. Decision making. 3. Group
facilitation.   I. Title.
HD66.P88 1998
658.3' 128--dc21   98-25716
                                                                  CIP

Published by
Deep Space Technology Company
P.O. Box 802
Bountiful, UT 84011-0802
(801) 292-1307   Fax (801) 292-0378

FACILITATION SKILLS
Helping
Groups
Make
Decisions

ABOUT THE AUTHOR

Gregory Putz has facilitated countless business, church, and civic groups over the past ten years. He is steadfast believer in the creative powers of groups and their abilities to solve problems.

Mr. Putz is a graduate of the University of California, Berkeley, and holds both Bachelor of Science and Master of Science degrees in Civil Engineering. He is a registered Professional Engineer in California and Utah.

Mr. Putz is a native of Santa Barbara, California, and currently lives with his wife, Suzanne, and his teenage daughters, Caroline and Danielle, in Bountiful, Utah.

PREFACE

Why do we need facilitation?

Because it enables any group to unlock the answers they are seeking. Those answers are the typically the root of change, either in a business or in some social'unit.

Unfortunately, society has encouraged an opposite approach. The popularity of individualism has discouraged active, group problem solving. Frequently, it is viewed as a weakness when one person seeks group involvement in selecting solutions.

Also, an individual or group typically waits for someone else to cause a change. This behavior is reinforced from childhood throughout our adult lives. If a solution exists then someone will give it to us. If change is to occur then someone else will initiate it. We are therefore conditioned to be reactive not proactive.

As a result, too often we look for change coming from the outside in... or from the top down. We typically wait for others to solve our problems. But to be truly successful, we must instead look within ourselves to find the true source of change. Simply said, the answers are within us.

This book helps find those answers.

As more businesses strive to become high perfor-mance organizations they will depend more and more upon the creative abilities of their employ-ees. As competitive pressures increase so will the demands upon employee work groups to de-velop and implement innovative solutions.

The traditional manager or supervisor can no longer provide answers to all the questions and demands of today's work place. With the techni-cal nature of business expanding so quickly, it will difficult for a manager to keep up. Simply said, tomorrow's manager or supervisor will not be able to solve every problem at the office. Business will increasingly rely on employee teams and work groups to implement innovative solutions to solve company problems.

And it will be the facilitation skills of both su-pervisors and non-supervisory employees that extract these innovation solutions from the work groups. Instead of the historically passive, di-rected work groups, business will see the evolu-tion of proactive, responsible ones. Such evolv-ing work groups will require the services of neutral facilitators to help them unlock their creative solutions.

This book shows how to do that. It provides both the process and insights necessary for any person to act as a neutral facilitator. This book outlines a step-by-step approach on how to help a work group unlock its creative abilities while main-taining a safe, positive atmosphere.

You need to study this book and apply its processes if you want to harness the creativity and innovation of your employees! The old days of command and control management are quickly disappearing. This book will give you the ability to help your work group focus on the issues, make decisions, and gain support for their actions! Why not start helping them today?

Gregory Bryan Putz
Bountiful, Utah
February 1998

CONTENTS

I. Steps for Successful Facilitation
 1 What's the **Issue**?

 2 What are Our **Concerns**?

 3 Any Possible **Solutions**?

 4 Our **Criteria**?

 5 What's Our **Action**?

 6 **Check**?

II. Doing It!
 7 Getting Started

 8 You and the Leader

 9 Pre-Meeting Logistics

 10 Flipcharts and Tools

 11 The Room

 12 The First Meeting

 13 Building Consensus

 14 Handling Conflict

III. Appendices
 15 Do's & Don'ts

 16 Frequently-Asked Questions

 17 Selected Resources

 18 Index

Respect the dignity,
the worth,
and
the creative potential
of
every human being
in the
organization.

Everyone
is
Welcome to Participate!

INTRODUCTION

Why facilitate?

Twenty years ago it was unheard of.

Ten years ago, facilitation was a rare activity.

Today, facilitation is a key to identifying problems, resolving misunderstanding, and creating action plans that groups can support... and, therefore, have an increased chance for success!

I have spent the past five years facilitating the needs of groups. The important word here is *needs*. Why?

Groups, individuals, teams, committees, councils... they all have needs. Needs to exist, needs to solve problems, needs to demonstrate a worthwhile reason for their existence within an organization.

Sometimes these needs are called goals or objectives or targets. And it's the facilitator who helps

these groups and its individuals act in an expe-
dient manner to fulfill these needs.

That is why facilitation is important.

And it's also why YOU can be a great help to the
success of any group, team, committee, or coun-
cil! Here are some key elements for a successful
facilitation process:

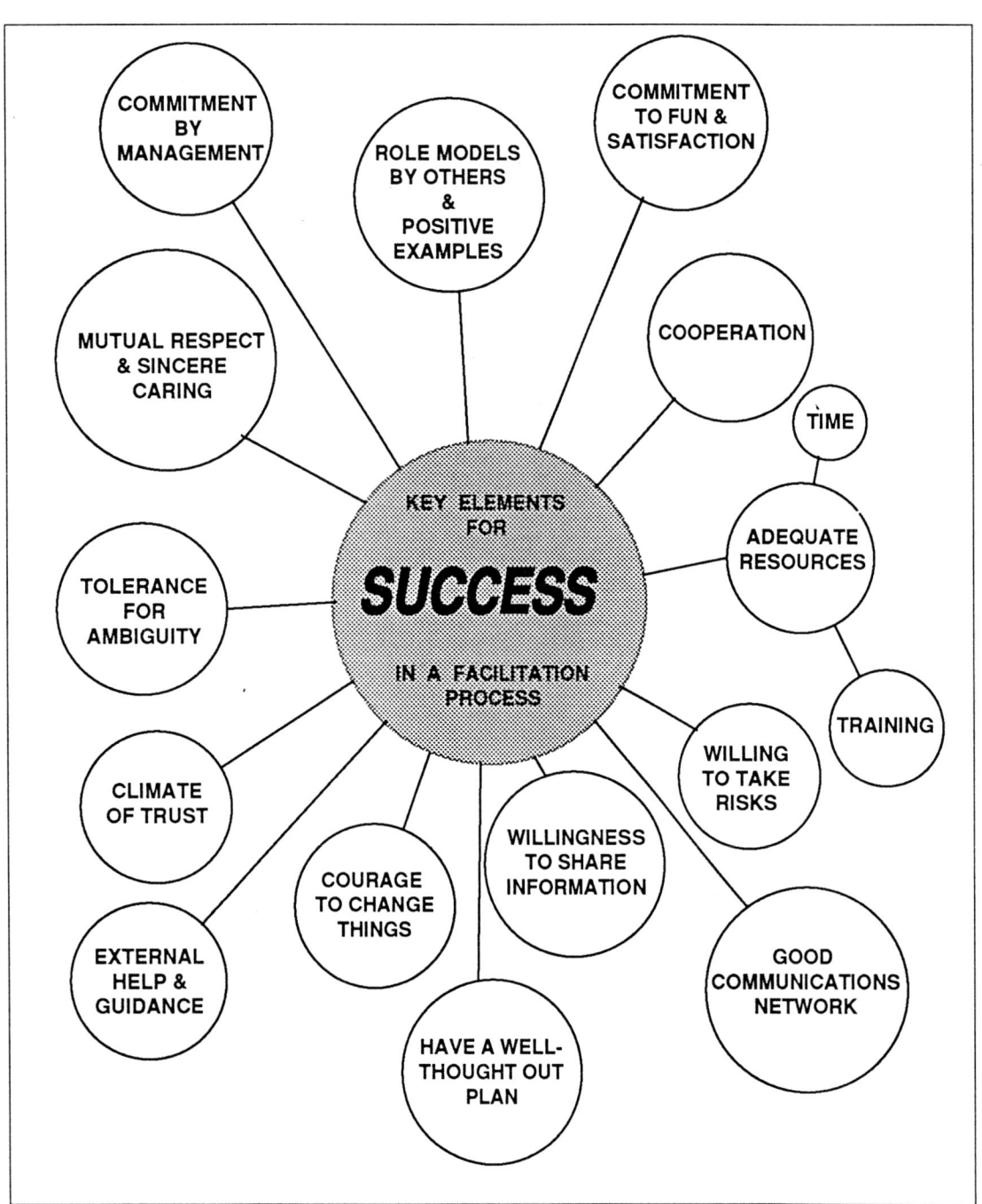

There are six steps to FACILITATION...

1   What is the **ISSUE** the group is trying to address?

2   What are the **CONCERNS** of each member of the group regarding this issue?

3   What are some **POSSIBILITIES** to solve the concerns?

4   What **CRITERIA** will the group use to judge each possibility?

5   What **ACTION** items will be selected from the list of possibilities?

6   **CHECK** to see if the action addresses the issue and the group's concerns.

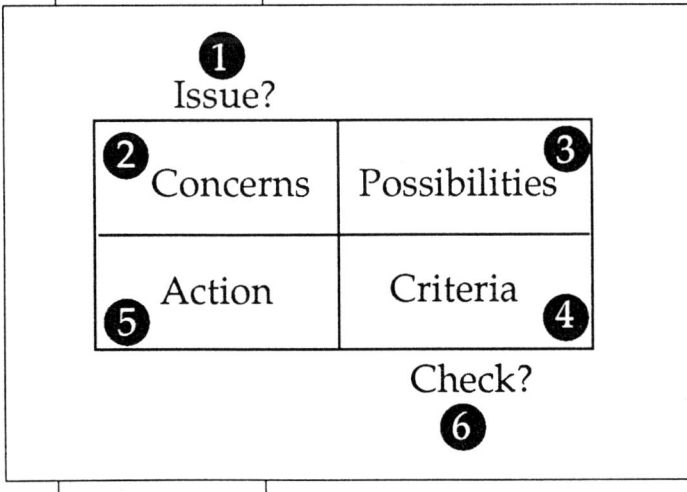

As a facilitator, I pledge...

- To be *fair*,
- To be *prepared* for each session,
- To *remain neutral* during all activities,
- To *help the group* come to some closure on the issue,
- To *seek the best* from each participant in the group,
- To make the process as *positively refinforcing* as possible.

ROLE OF THE FACILITATOR

The facilitator is a neutral servant of any group. He or she focuses the energy of the group towards a common goal. Part of the facilitiator's job is also handling the logistics before the meetings and afterwards.

The facilitator owns the process. The group owns the content. Accordingly, the facilitator makes suggestions and judgments and takes action in regard to the procedures and sequencing of group events, or the process. He or she does not evaluate ideas, or the content, created by the group. In all cases, the facilitator seeks to find a win-win situation.

Another important job is protecting individuals within the group from attack. A facilitator assures that the playing field is level and everyone has an equal opportunity to participate.

The facilitator is there to help the group succeed.

A facilitator is neutral

A Facilitator is...

- **Enthusiastic** about causing positive change through team action!

- A **salesperson** for the concept of team problem-solving!

- A **role model** and **mentor** for others in the area of facilitation and team problem-solving!

- **Brave** and not afraid of groups!

- **Willing to help others** solve their problems!

Facilitator helps the group and remains neutral

The facilitator owns the process.

The group owns the content.

The organization owns the results.

And the organization also owns the responsibility to provide the facilitator and the group all the support necessary to make them a success.

And to be a success, there are three fundamental requirements that everyone shares responsibility for:

- The group must have a **clear purpose**

- The participants need to be **committed** to the purpose, to the process, and have some benefit from, or stake in, the outcome

- The process must be given **adequate resources** (time, money, manpower, support) for its successful completion

CONTENT

(GROUP OWNS IT)

<u>WHAT</u> the group has to accomplish...

- Agenda
- Issue
- Job
- Decisions
- Action Items
- Plans
- Assignments

PROCESS

(YOU OWN IT)

<u>HOW</u> the group works together...

- Involvement
- Trust
- Openness
- Pace
- Equality
- Sequence of tasks
- Checks & Validations

Get these points resolved at the first meeting

What is the scope of this task?	• What is the purpose of this group? • What is the problem? • What are the limits? Boundaries?
What is authority level of this group?	• Gather information only? • Recommend action? • Decide? • Implement?
What does success look like?	• What is the goal of this process? • How will we know when we are done? • What will the final product look like?
What are the critical elements in the process?	• How will we agree? By consensus? Voting? • Who are the stakeholders regarding the issue? • What communication methods will the group use to keep outsiders informed?
What is the timing?	• What is the deadline? • What happens if the group goes longer?
What are the roles of the participants?	• Why is each person here? • What is expected of each person? • Will each member express his/her own ideas... or will the member represent the ideas of people outside the group? • Who is missing from this group?

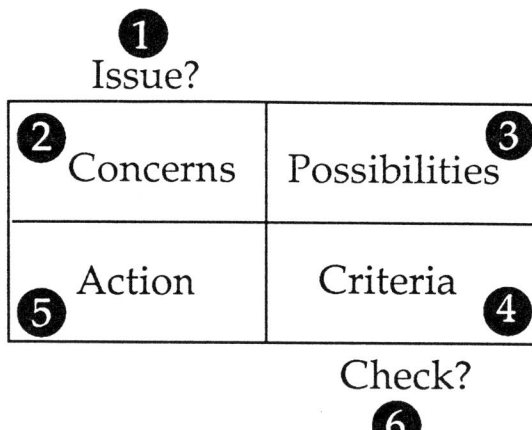

I

Steps for Successful Facilitation

1. Issue?
2. Concerns?
3. Possible Solutions?
4. Criteria?
5. Action?
6. Check?

1 ISSUE?

What's the issue?

How often we forget to ask!

Committees, teams, and groups typically form to address some problem, concern, or issue. That's not uncommon. What is troublesome, however, is that if no one asks the obvious question "Why are we here?" at the meeting's start it could become embarrassing later... or worse!

As a facilitator, assume that nothing is a "given" or common knowledge to all the participants. A quick poll of people in the room can quickly sort out any differences of opinion over the purpose or subject of the session.

If differences arise, then work with the group to agree on what single issue they would like to address at today's session. Major topics that fall outside that issue can be recorded on an "Issues Bin" sheet on the room wall and addressed at another meeting.

If the group cannot agree on the issue, then stop and adjourn. At that point, consult the Leader for direction and reschedule another meeting.

WHAT'S THE ISSUE?

(1) **Ask the group, "What's the issue?"** Go around the room and have each person give his or her idea of today's issue.

(2) **Write down each person's comment.** Use a flipchart soeveryone can see.

(3) **Find any common elements of the ideas written on the flipchart.** Circle identical words or phrases. Have the group help you.

(4) **Build a draft issue statement.** Use a clean flipchart sheet. Look at the circled words and phrases on the other flipchart. Using these common ideas, write a draft issue. *Warning: Avoid the trap of writing a solution statement instead of an issue statement.*

(5) **Have the group help you revise the draft statement.** Cross out words. Add words. Rearrange words. It's OK to end up with a messy flipchart but make sure that the groups helps you make the changes!

(6) **Ask the group, "Is this the issue?"** Have them look at the revised issue statement you've written on the flipchart. Allow plenty of time for everyone to think about it. Make any suggested changes to your draft issue statement.

(7) **Get the group to agree.** One last time, ask the group if they can all support the issue as written on the flipchart. If not, find out what has to be changed to

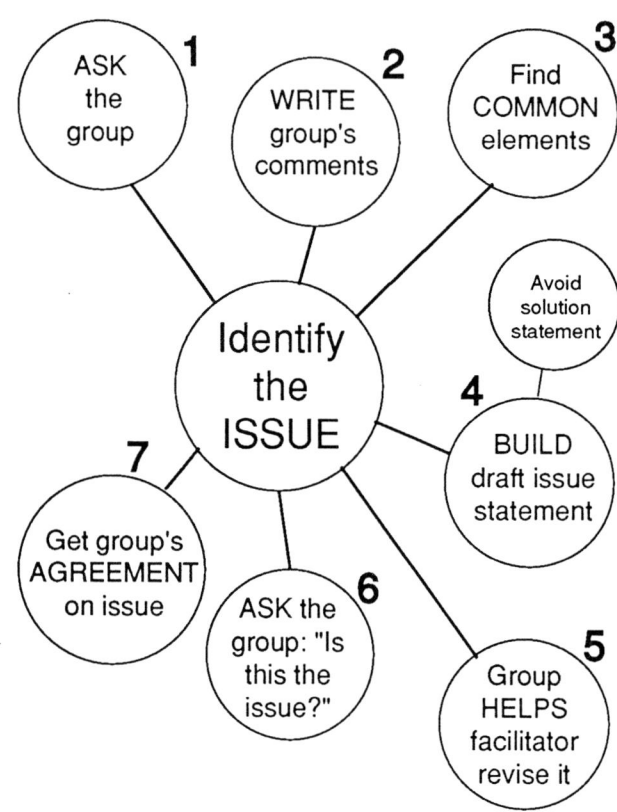

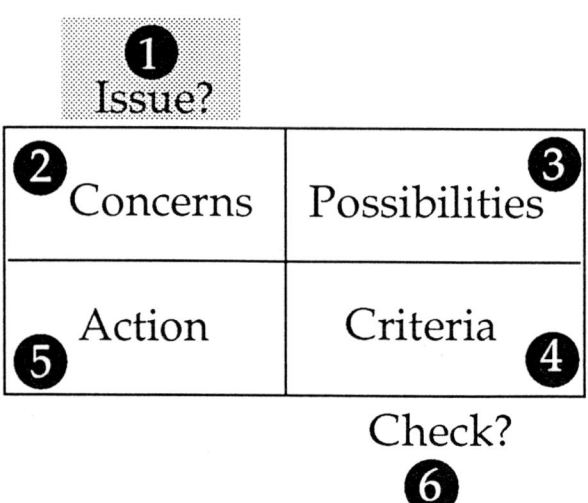

Case Study: What's the Issue?

Background

The random drug testing team had their first meeting on Tuesday. During this two hour session, Tom, the facilitator, reviewed the management's instructions to the team, discussed the key stakeholders, and gathered everyone's *concerns*.

The team met for three more meetings during the following weeks. Tom had the group brainstorm *possibilities* and agree on a list of *criteria*. During the fifth meeting, the random drug testing team developed specific *action items* (in the form of recommendations to management) using their lists of possibilities and criteria.

Half way through this fifth session Tom had to adjourn the group early because it became polarized over the wording of the recommendations. Half the group wanted to recommend punishment for those employees failing to take or pass the Company's random drug tests. The balance wanted to recommend steps in the procedure of administering random drug testing at the plant and not address nature of any punishment. Each side argued for the validity of their recommendations.

The Problem

Tom saw that this team was deadlocked. Neither faction would acknowledge the recommendations of the other. After five meetings the team was nowhere near consensus on any output. What had happened?

It is clear that the team was not clear on the issue. A common error, everyone assumed that everyone else held the same definition of the issue. Tom did not take the time initially to review the issue with the group. He assumed that everyone knew the "random drug testing" meant "creating a plant policy on conducting random drug testing." After all, that was the instruction given to him from the management team.

What Happened?

Tom had assumed wrong.

At the sixth meeting Tom polled the membership and was surprised at the variety of responses to his question, "What do you think the issue is?"

Yvette said, "The issue is 'Making sure everyone complies with the new random drug testing program'."

Eddy said, "Keeping our plant drug free!"

Jack said, "Getting employees to live healthier by avoiding drugs and alcohol."

Tom, as facilitator, should have made the team agree at the first meeting on the issue. Once they agreed on a single issue future disagreements would have been avoided.

The Lesson

Do these steps at your *first meeting*:

(**1**) Poll the room asking, "What do you think the issue is?"

(**2**) Write each response on a flipchart.

(**3**) Rewrite the responses into a single Issue Statement.

(**4**) Get the group's consensus (edit the Issue Statement as required).

(**5**) Post the Issue Statement on the wall.

(**6**) Refer back to the Issue Statement throughout the facilitation process.

ISSUE

OUR ISSUE IS:

Creating a plant policy on conducting random drug testing.

Ways to Promote Participation

- Make eye-contact with the person

- Ask questions that are "open-ended"

- Use silence

- Make comments reinforcing participants and cause members to ac
  knowledge each other

- Call directly on a person

- Post key ideas or statements on the wall

- Create the expectation that members come prepared

- Avoid interventions that are "win-lose" and seek "win-win" ones

- Share with the group your participation expectations of them

- Lighten up and use humor

- Be positive and non-judgemental

- Give your attention to the speaker

- Use proper body language

2 CONCERNS?

How do you **feel** about this issue?

What are you **concerned** about? What do you **think** about this issue?

Gathering the concerns of each individual in the group is very important. It provides each person an opportunity to explore his or her feelings about the issue at hand.

There is no judgement of anyone's thoughts and feelings during this step in the process. You as the facilitator need to be active in discouraging comments and discussions.

All concerns should be recorded on a flipchart and hung on the walls of the meeting room. They will be used later in Step 6 when the team checks its action items to assure that they address the issue... and the concerns of the group.

Gathering concerns is an important step in facilitation process for two reasons. First, it forces each member of the group to focus on the issue. And second, it provides a helpful reference during the brainstorming of solutions.

Guidelines for gathering concerns

• Concerns are the thoughts, feelings, reflections, and impressions of each member of the group. *They are not how someone else feels or thinks about the issue.* Concerns are personal.

• Concerns always begin with "I think..." or "I feel..." or "I'm concerned about..."

• There should be no debate, no criticism, nor any challenges to a person's concern. Period.

• Start off by offering an example. Then ask for a volunteer for the first concern. Go around the room asking each member for one concern... keep going until the group is finished.

• Don't put anyone in an awkward situation... just tell them "It's OK if you'd like to pass on this round."

• After you write a person's concern on the flipchart sheet, ask them to read it and then ask "Is this what you mean?"

• Post the flipchart sheets because you'll need them in Step Three during the brainstorming of possibilities.

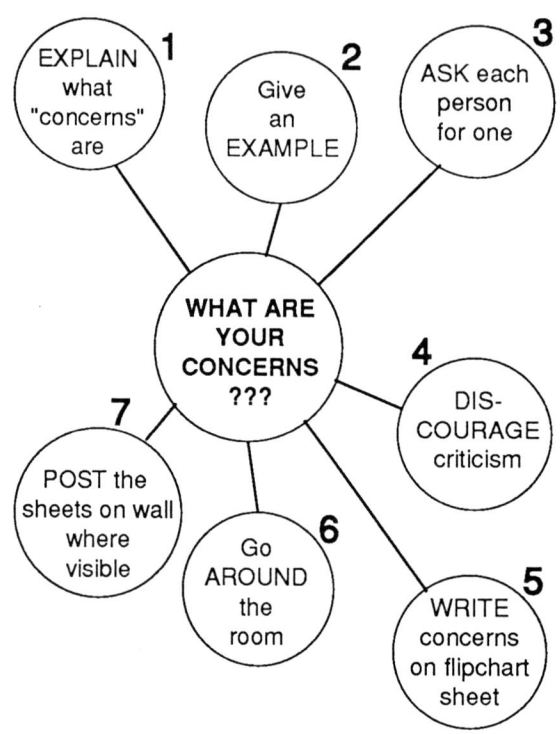

❶
Issue?

❷ Concerns	Possibilities ❸
Action ❺	Criteria ❹

Check?

Case Study: What are your concerns?

Background

Will was quiet most of the time. Dedicated to his routine duties, Will worked in the Purchasing Department as a clerk for the past eight years. He was cooperative with fellow workers but never a person to speak his mind in public.

Judy, his supervisor, had called a meeting today to resolve a long-standing problem within the group: errors in entering data into the department's shipping records. She was concerned that both the shipping and receiving clerks were being careless. Despite her coaching of individuals on the correct procedures, many errors were still being made.

Tom, the facilitator, began the meeting in the usual way. He announced to the group his role as a neutral facilitator and reviewed the process that they would follow. After the group agreed on their boundaries, rules, and stakeholders, Tom reviewed the issue with them and obtained the group's consensus on the issue statement.

Tom next gathered concerns from the group. Before starting, he reiterated that *concerns were the thoughts, feelings, reflections, and impressions* of each person in the room regarding the issue. There is no right or wrong concern and, so, no criticism permitted during this step of the process.

Tom started with the first person on his right. Tara, a shipping clerk, boldly said, "I'm concerned that no matter what we do, it'll never be good enough for management." The next person in the circle, Josh, said, "I think that our computer equipment and software is outdated and isn't the right stuff to have!"

After collecting the concerns of several more people, Tom could tell Judy was becoming angry. Her body language and facial expressions clearly telegraphed impatience. Tom continued around the room to Will, who quietly said, "I'm concerned that we have so much work that we can't enter the data correctly even if we wanted to." Finally, Judy exploded by saying, "That's not true! That's simply not true!" Will immediately slumped down in this chair and stared at the floor.

Tom went on to the next person, who said, "Pass." And the next person, who said, "I'll pass." And the next said the same. And the next, too. Tom looked back at Judy and said nothing. She looked bewildered.

The Problem

Tom knew that any trust in the room had evaporated with Judy's outburst.

Members of the group were no longer willing to share their feeling and thoughts about the issue. Judy knew that she had spoken out of turn and she had criticized Will's feelings. The "safe zone" offered by the facilitation process was gone. Any openness within the meeting was gone, also.

What Happened?

Tom allowed Judy to criticize Will's concern. *By doing so, Tom actions said to group "Hey - it's OK for the boss to criticize you in this meeting... so you better be careful what you say!"*

Tom should have *immediately* stopped Judy by saying, "Judy, our process does not allow any criticism of concerns." Then Tom should have reinforced his words by pointing to the wall where a flipchart was taped, saying "Rule #6 - No criticism of concerns or possibilities".

The Lesson

Not only did Will stop talking but the entire group also stopping sharing their feelings. *And Tom lost some of his credibility as a neutral facilitator.*

Experience has shown that almost always *people only want an opportunity to express what's on their minds.* It's as simple as that. Too often, supervisors and managers are afraid that groups will use facilitated sessions to promote actions that are contrary to the welfare of the business. Again, experience has shown that they don't. People only want a chance to say what's on their minds. And collecting concerns is a step that provides each person with a safe, non-judgmental environment to express their inner feelings.

So, why is expressing these inner feelings so important to the process? First, it gives people like Will, who are reticent but *may* have a helpful perspective on the issue, an opportunity to share a unique point of view. Second, it provides a stage, or even a "soapbox", for team members to once-and-for-all tell the group (and the supervisor!) how they really feel... and then be finished. Third, it provides a checklist to verify that the group's action will satisfy the concerns of the group.

When you facilitate a group, do the following items during the *concerns* step:

(1) Tell the group, "Concerns are your personal thoughts, feelings, or reflections. They are *your* concerns... *not someone else's* concerns."

(2) Reinforce the rule of no criticism.

(3) Suggest that each person express her or his concern starting with "I feel..." or "I think..." or "I'm concerned about...".

(4) If anyone says "I disagree..." or "I don't think so..." or any other form of criticism - STOP THEM IMMEDIATELY! Any criticism at this point of the process is a plague that causes silence and it spreads like wildfire!

(5) Be careful that <u>you</u> as facilitator don't criticize! After a person offers a concern don't respond by saying, "That's good" or "Good thought" or "Great!". *Remember: criticism can be positive as well as a negative!*

CONCERNS

OUR CONCERNS
ABOUT THE ISSUE:

- I worry about....
- I feel that....
- I think....
- I'm concerned about...

3

POSSIBLE SOLUTIONS?

People working in groups can create an amazing number of possible solutions. Far more, I believe, than an individual can alone.

Possible solutions, or possibilities, are the foundation for new and creative approaches to addressing the issue. Open, free-wheeling brainstorming is an easy and fun way for groups to generate numerous innovative answers.

As the third step in the facilitation process, developing possibilities is the most energizing. The facilitator should shepard the process with lots of ENERGY! This is an opportunity for the facilitator to be a role model... get excited, be energetic, and throw out a few examples to "seed" the group's thoughts. Increase your tempo, be upbeat, and challenge individuals to suggest the craziest ideas on how to solve the problem!

These possibilities will be the basis for your action items in Step Five. So encourage the group to generate as many ideas as possible. Remember... anything goes! And no judging of ideas! And no criticism of ideas!

Let's go!

Brainstorming is one way to get a group's synergy into full production creating new and previously unconsidered solutions.

Start this step by explaining the rules:

> • One person speaks at a time
> • No criticism of other people's ideas
> • OK to ask for clarification of an idea
> • Building upon ideas is encouraged

Use a flipchart to record the possibilities.

Don't get caught in the trap of analyzing any possibility "as to whether or not it pertains to the issue." That is judging. Just write down the individual's suggestion and keep moving! In Step Four, the group's criteria will sort out any possibilities not addressing the issue... for now, you want to keep up the momentum and keep people popping out ideas!

Keep the pace snappy! Throw out some ideas of your own as an example to help the group along.

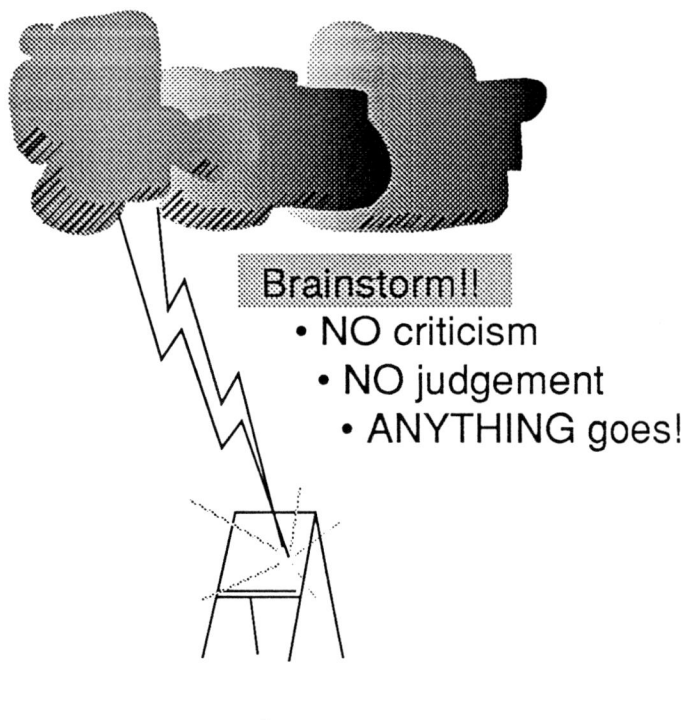

Brainstorm!!
• NO criticism
• NO judgement
• ANYTHING goes!

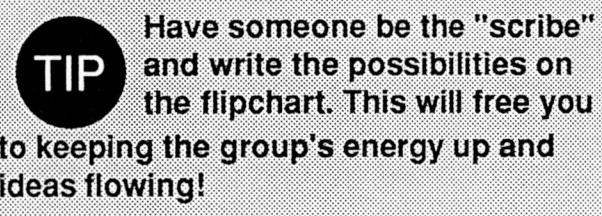

TIP Have someone be the "scribe" and write the possibilities on the flipchart. This will free you to keeping the group's energy up and ideas flowing!

❶
Issue?

❷ Concerns	Possibilities ❸
Action ❺	Criteria ❹

Check?
❻

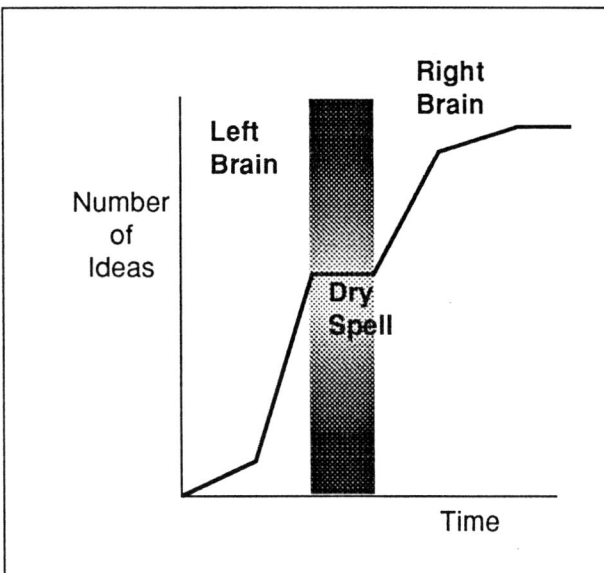

How Groups Brainstorm Ideas Over Time

Ideas from a group come in phases.

During the first phase, individuals draw solutions from their logic. This involves looking at the issue or problem and developing an answer from an analytical perspective. We commonly call this a "left brain" approach; that is, solutions are a result of a sequential analysis of the problem. This is a very natural way for most people to solve problems.

During this first phase, you as facilitator will be given many "common sense" solutions. Typically there will be nothing too surprising or too radical presented by the group.

Soon these possibilities using logical solutions will trickle to an end. And then there will be silence in the room. Don't be fooled into stopping this process step by saying, "Well, I guess that's all the possibilities!"

Instead, allow for the silence to continue. Wait several minutes if necessary. It may be uncomfortable, but there is something going on within the heads of each individual in the room.

At this point, everyone in the group has exhausted his or her inventory of logical, left-brained ideas. So, now the logical (left) part of the brain is soliciting input from the emotional and creative (right) side. Hence, silence in the room!

Soon, you as facilitator will be given another spurt of very creative possibilities! Now the group is pouring forth wacky, crazy ideas by using the right-side of their brains. By waiting through the group's silence, you now have tapped the creative side of the group. People will offer some strangle possibilities... and then others in the room will build on them! Great!! Keep the momentum going at a quick pace until you drain every idea from the team.

> **TIP** Explain to the group how the left and right sides of the brain contribute ideas during this process. Warn the group that there will be a period of silence and that it is a very natural occurrence.

DRY SPELLS HAPPEN! SILENCE IS OK!

Types of Brainstorming

Free Wheeling

- also known as "Popcorn" method
- group members call out ideas
- write ideas on flipchart as they
  are suggested

Round Robin

- also known as "Going Around the Room"
- facilitator asks members for ideas in order
- OK for anyone to "pass"
- write ideas on flipchart as they
  are suggested

Paper Method

- also known as "Write Down Your Ideas"
- group members write ideas on index cards
  or slips of paper or 3M Post-It™ notes
- one idea per piece of paper
- facilitator tapes or sticks pieces of paper on
  flipchart sheet (avoid re-writing them!)

Rules for Brainstorming!!

Build on the ideas of others!

Make ideas clear and talk in "headlines"

Encourage everyone to participate!

Don't judge, criticize, or evaluate ideas!

Have fun! Get those creative juices flowing!

Write down every idea... no matter how crazy!

Generate as many ideas as possible... strive for a large QUANTITY of possibilities!

Case Study: What are the possibilities?

Background

Owen was brilliant. But he never learned how to shut up.

Owen was the current leader of the plant's Control Support Team. Being the chief CST member was a big responsibility because plant profitability was a direct result of the control computer's operation. He worked with nine other CST members, all providing 24 hour technical support for plant operators.

Several months ago, a management consultant met with the CST to conduct upwards-feedback sessions. One of the outputs of these sessions was the recommendation to create better relations between the CST and internal customers. Acting on this recommendation, Owen called Tom to facilitate a meeting of the team to decide on how to improve customer relations.

At one o'clock Tom began the meeting. Eight CST members were in attendance including Owen. Tom quickly moved through the preliminary elements of issue, stakeholders, communications, and concerns. Within an hour of the meeting's start, Tom had began brainstorming possibilities.

After fifteen minutes of round-robin brainstorming, the group fell quiet. Tom felt the uneasiness in the room but purposely said nothing.

"Come on, Tom," Owen said, finally cracking the silence. "Let's hurry up and get through this!" His impatience was undisguised as he continued, "We've all done this before, Tom. What's the delay?"

Tom was about to respond but Owen spoke first.

"We've got a turnover meeting in thirty minutes. The next shift will be coming on and we've got to be there during the turnover," Owen blurted out. "Can't we end this brainstorming now?"

Everyone stared at Owen. No one said a word.

The Problem

Tom now realized that Owen had a time constraint previously unknown to him. It governed Owen's perception of the meeting's timing and caused him to lash out at the facilitator when things were going too slowly. Sadly, Tom was never told about it and was catch off-guard.

Any creative spirit in the room was now gone. Owen's impatient outburst not only violated several meeting rules but also squelched the group's upbeat feelings, or eustress, that is essential for brainstorming.

What Happened?

Reflecting on the day later that evening, Tom determined that two key elements caused the breakdown in the facilitation. First, Owen's anxiety over attending the turnover meeting overpowered his need to appear supportive of the facilitation process. Second, Owen failed to share with Tom the need to finish the session before the two-thirty Operations turnover meeting.

The Lesson

After additional reflection that evening, Tom made a mental note to himself of things he would do in the future:

1. During the pre-meeting discussion with the leader, he would ask the leader if there are any time limits on the sessions. *And not ask it just once but several times...* to be certain the leader hasn't forgotten anything.

2. If ever interrupted by someone during a meeting (like Owen's outburst) over the facilitation process, *he would announce a short time-out*. Not only would this recess pro vide an opportunity to discuss any difficulties but the intermission would help "cool off" the interrupter.

3. If a solution couldn't be reached during the time-out then the facilitation process should be adjourned and another meeting time set to continue the process. Why? *If the disruption to the group's brainstorming was significant enough, then it would be very difficult to restore the eustress in the room.* The best plan would be let any hostilities subside and start the brainstorming again later.

> "Men and melons are hard to know."
> **- Benjamin Franklin,**
> *Poor Richard's Almanac*

4 CRITERIA?

This is an important step.

These criteria set the group's boundaries of acceptable action. Any brainstormed possibility that fails to satisfy the criteria cannot become an action item.

It is important that the group be flexible and be willing to revisit its criteria list. As the group's discussion proceeds, individuals will discover that either some criterion is not realistic or that additional ones are needed.

You as the facilitator should challenge the group to closely examine the validity of any criterion adopted.

The group's criteria list "sets the stage" for determining action steps necessary to address the issue. They also help the group explain to outsiders and stakeholders the rationale of why (or why not) the group choose specific actions.

Basic Criteria

Whatever the group decides to do, that action must:

* Be legal and moral
* Be achievable
* Be understandable to all others
* Meet the needs of the issue
* Recognize limited resources available

TIP Start with the Basic Criteria and ask the group if they would like to add or delete criterion. If the group is at a loss for other criteria, suggest some criterion from the advanced list.

Criteria act as the "strainer" for the group's possibilities. Those possibilities that meet the criteria will "pass through" and become action items.

It is during this exercise that the group may realize that their criteria list is incorrect or imcomplete. You as the facilitator should accomodate any changes in the criteria list that the group desires.

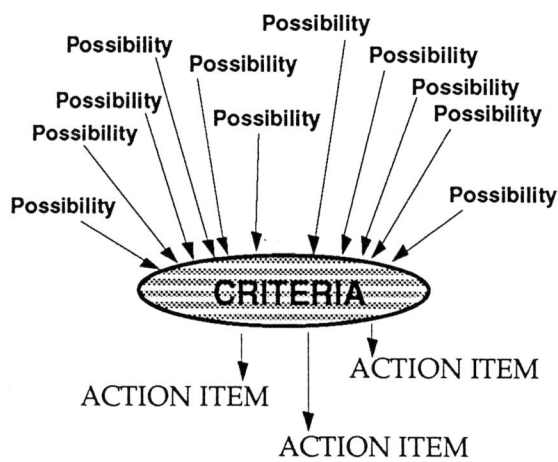

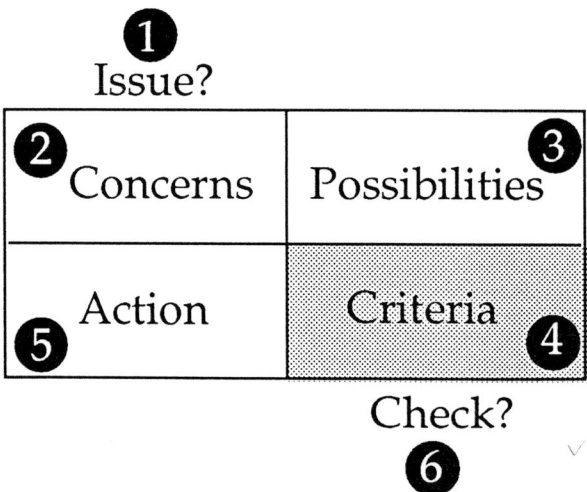

Advanced Criteria

Whatever the group decides to do, that action must:

✳ Support and be consistent with our organization's vision & mission

✳ Consider the adverse impact on ourselves and on others

✳ Be cost effective

✳ Have a clear owner

✳ Have results which are measurable

✳ Meet any contractual obligations

✳ Allow for input from concerned individuals and organizations

✳ Address long-term implications as well as short-term needs

✳ Have a clear focus

✳ Consider a life cycle - when does it end?

✳ Recognize company needs and strategies

✳ Be manageable

✳ Have customer approval and buy-in

✳ Be K.I.S.S. - as least complex as possible

✳ Add value

✳ Be consistent and fair to all persons involved

✳ Incorporate some feedback process

✳ Cause resolution of the problem in a timely manner

Creating the Group's Criteria List

Step One

•Use the **Basic Criteria** and **Advanced Criteria** lists as resources for suggesting possible criterion to the group.

Step Two

•List all possible criterion suggested by the group.

Step Three

•Use consensus-building tools to obtain the group's final Criteria List.

Possible Criterion - p. 2

- helps get me promoted
- is legal & moral
- has clear owner
- has customer buy-in
- supports Co. mission
- supports our vision
- adds value
- manageable
- incorporates feedback

Possible Criterion - p. 3

- has an end to it
- passes "bulletin-board test"
- is simple
- can be measured
- fair to everyone
- cost effective
- does not violate any Company policies

Possible Criterion - p. 1

- makes money
- achievable
- understandable to all?
- meets customers' needs?
- allows us to have fun?
- no impact on budget
- supports union contract

Our CRITERIA

Whatever we do, it will...
- be legal & moral
- satisfy the customers' needs
- be cost-effective
- meet Company policies

Case Study: What are our criteria?

Background

Tom stood at the flipchart easel with his back to the group. Turning his head to face them, he asked, "OK, let's list some criteria for deciding our action. Anyone want to start?"

Silence. He turned and faced them. He repeated, "Anyone? Any criteria or rules to judge our possibilities?"

Enough of the room looked lost that Tom stopped. He put the marker pen down and walked to the center of the room.

"I sense that no one has the energy to keeping going," he said. "Should we stop for today? We can meet tomorrow at one o'clock."

No one spoke.

Curious, Tom looked at Sandy and asked, "Sandy, what would you like to do now?"

For the first time since Tom's monologue began she looked at Tom and replied, "I'm lost. I don't know what we should be doing now... I mean, how are we going to sort through eight flipcharts of possibilities?"

"Yeah. It's just too overwhelming, Tom," Burt called out from the back of the room, "we've got all these possibilities and we're no closer to solving our problem than when we started!"

Tom nodded his head. "I understand," he said. "Let's take a fifteen minute break... be back at two forty-five."

The Problem

Many, if not all, of the team members were *frustrated* with their progress towards solving the problem outlined in their issue statement. They had lost sight of the process steps following the brainstorming of the possibilities step.

What Happened?

Tom was embarrassed with himself because he had assumed the group understood the importance of the *criteria step*. They did not.

Pulling open his facilitation binder, he found a list of possible criteria for the group. He wrote several of them on a blank flipchart sheet:

- Measurable
- Legal & moral
- Not cause us to exceed our expense budget
- Satisfies Company policies
-
-
-

These would serve as "seeds" for the group to create their own list of criteria. The three bullets with blanks afterwards would be spaces he'd write in the group's own criteria.

At two forty-five, Tom re-started the meeting by announcing, "Here's a sample list of criteria for us to consider." He pointed to the flipchart he'd prepared during the break. "Please read them."

Tom continued, "OK, now. Remember that the criteria you select will be the rules, or test, for each of the possibilities. If any possibility doesn't meet the criteria then it can't become part of the group's action plan."

"Questions?" he asked. "Great. Sandy, finish this sentence for me: *'Whatever we do, it will...'* "

Sandy winced. After a few moments she replied, "...meet the operating guidelines of the plant." She immediately repeated, "Whatever we do will meet the operating guidelines of the plant."

"Good!" Tom said, "Now, Burt, you finish the same sentence for us: *'Whatever we do, it will...'* "

The Lesson

Take the time to explain the concept of criteria to the group. Too often, facilitators assume that everyone understands this process step. Although all human beings use criteria constantly during their waking hours to decide personal actions, we forget how to purposely apply them in formal facilitations.

Do this during the criteria step:

(1) Explain how the group's *criteria is important* to sorting out its possibilities.

(2) Show some *example criteria* from a standard list.

(3) Prime the group for their suggestions by *phrasing your question* as, "Whatever we do, it will..."

(4) After listing everyone's suggestions for criteria, start at the top of the list and *obtain their consensus* for each one. If the group can't support a criteria, then discard it.

(5) Don't be surprised if, as the action items are being built in the following step, *the group wishes to revise its list of criteria* and go back to reconsider some previously discarded possibilities. *This desire is natural* and reassessing criteria, at any time, is an acceptable process step.

Our <u>CRITERIA</u>

Whatever we do, it will...
- be legal & moral
- satisfy the customers' needs
- be cost-effective
- meet Company policies

5

ACTION?

Action is the desired output of nearly every group.

In our society, we have a bias towards action and, unfortunately, most groups jump from *concerns* (Step Two) directly to *action* (Step Five) without the benefits of (1) identifying the issue, (2) brainstorming possibilities for solutions, or (3) agreeing on the criteria for selecting the action items. Such haste typically results in action that fails to solve the problem and forces the group to spend more time later trying to develop some other plan of attack to rectify the issue.

This process avoids that problem. After a group agrees on its criteria in Step Four, it is then possible to screen the list of possibilities for acceptable solutions. By applying the criteria to each possibility generated in Step Three, the group creates a list of potential action items.

What to do...

1 • Hang the possibilities flipchart sheets on a wall in front of the group

2 • Start with the first possibility. Ask the group "Does this possibility satisfy our criteria?"

3 • If the group agrees that it satisfies the criteria then quickly move on to the next possibility and repeat the question.

4 • If the group does not agree that the possibility meets the criteria, then cross-out the item and move on to the next one.

5 • After going through the entire list of possibilities, go back and group together any that are similar.

6 • After completing this grouping, select one group and build an action item.

7 • Continue building action items from the groups until finished. Remember that action items answer "what", "who", and "when".

8 • The next step is to check your action against the concerns raised in Step Two.

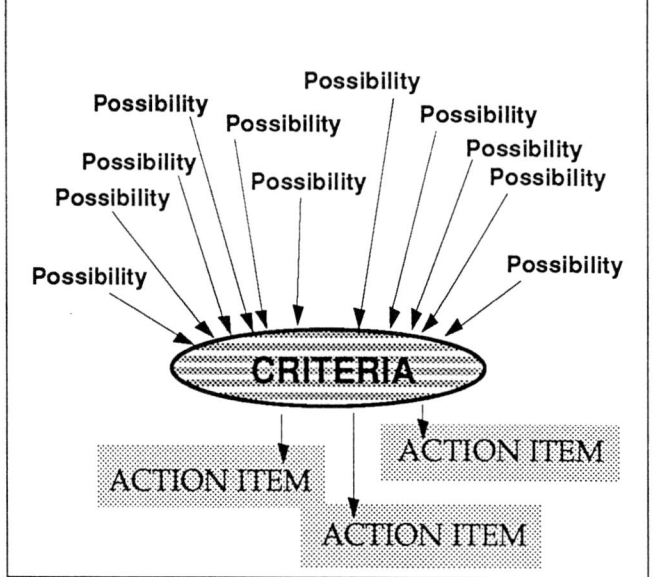

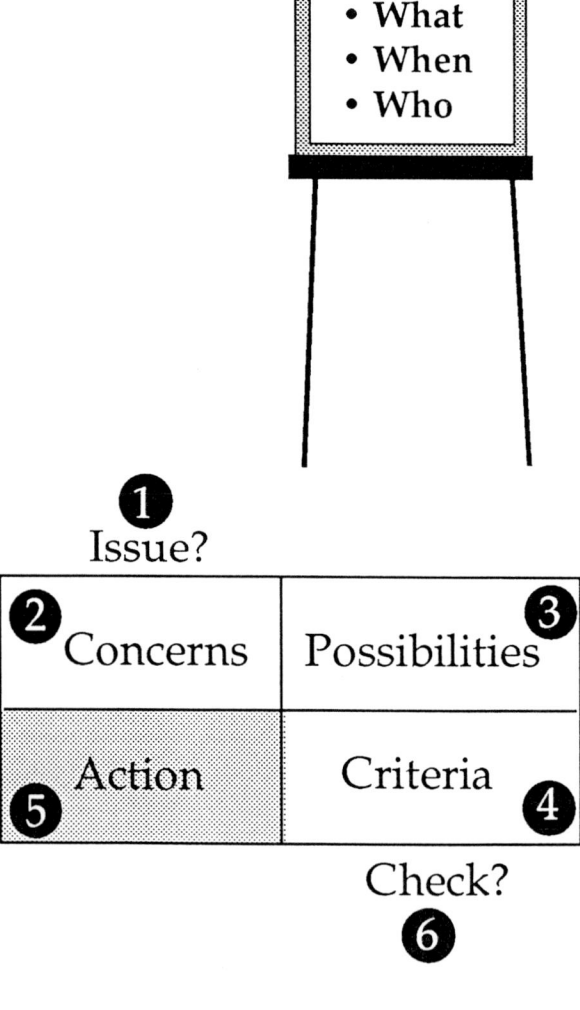

Case Study: What's our action plan?

Background

The group was returning from a fifteen minute break. Three of the team members were standing near the door talking.

"This is really stupid, Tom. We've spent three meetings on this issue and all we have to show for it are twelve pages of alternatives!" Hal complained.

"If you had listened at the start of all this, Hal, then you'd know that we won't do *each* of them," Brenda interrupted. "We'll only do the ones that meeting our criteria."

"It's no different than how you decided what to do in your own life, Hal," Barry quipped, "you have dozens of criteria that you use to sort out what's your next step."

"Yeah," Brenda added, "like when you're trying to decide what to buy for lunch."

"What?" Hal winced as he countered, "how does my buying lunch have anything to do with solving our group's issue? You guys aren't making any sense!"

"Look here," Tom interjected, "Brenda and Barry have a important point. Let's use the group's criteria to eliminate the unacceptable possibilities."

"What do you mean?" Hal asked.

"Remember the list of criteria we just agreed on? You know, those statements saying 'Whatever we do, it will be legal and moral,' or '...it won't cause us to exceed our budget'," Tom said.

"I remember them clearly. But those are just our rules for whatever action we take, right?" Hal replied.

"Right! And to make sure of that, we use those criteria as tests for *each* of our possibilities. We'll go down the list of possibilities, all twelve pages of them, and test each one against the criteria. If a possibilities doesn't satisfy all of our criteria we'll cross it off!" Tom instructed.

"OK. I see the value in doing that. But then what'll we do with the possibilities that made it through the criteria. Do we build action items out of them?" Hal asked.

"Bingo! Now you understand, Hal!" Brenda chimed it. "We'll take the possibilities that pass the criteria test and build action items out of them!"

"And remember what Tom told us... action items need to be specific, have an owner, and a time limit!" Barry added.

"Now I understand! Let's start building some action items!" Hal responded.

Tom called the team back together and announced that it was time to start building some action items.

"The vice president of manufacturing asked that we provide the plant management team with a list of specific tasks this team proposes to do to solve the issue. Are we ready to start converting all of our brainstormed possibilities into some action?" Tom asked.

"Let's do it!" Hal yelled with a smile.

The Problem
Hal, and maybe others in the group, felt overwhelmed because of the large quantity of possible solutions generated in the process. After several days of work, he and others felt no closer to solving the issue than at the start of the process. His frustration was obvious.

If not immediately addressed, Hal's frustration could have undermined the effectiveness of the team. Tom had seen this happen before when one or more team members who cannot see the connection between the possibilities, criteria, and action item steps become openly critical of the process.

What Happened?
Tom, as the facilitator, assumed that everyone understood the process steps necessary to reduce the possibilities into action items. At least one person, and possibly others, did not. *Tom should have spent more time repeating the steps of the process to assure that everyone understood.* Because experienced facilitators do the possibilities-criteria-action item sequence so frequently, they can mistakenly assume that everyone knows it equally well.

The Lesson

Do this: *three times* during the facilitation process remind the group of how action items are made : (1) *at the beginning* when first explaining the process, (2) once again *after brainstorming of possibilities*, and (3) finally, *after finishing the criteria step.*

When reminding the group, cover these three points:

(1) Action Items are made of one or more possibilities *that satisfy the group's criteria.*

(2) Action Items are the *final output* of the group. They are tasks involving activity by one or more people, usually group members.

(3) Action Items must have three components: *what, who, & when.*
    What = specific task to be completed
    Who = person responsible for completion of the task
    When = latest date when the task must be completed

ACTION ITEMS		
What	Who	When

6

CHECK?

How do you know that your actions will address the issue?

In this final step, you as facilitator will lead the group in reviewing each action item to assure it addresses the concerns of the group. It is usually a *quick step* and creates the *final closure* needed before the group adjourns and begins to implement the action items.

Simply ask the group, "Does these action items address our issue and your concerns?" With the concerns flipchart sheets posted on the wall before the group, allow sufficient time for the group to read the concerns again.

If there are concerns not addressed by the action items, ask the group, "Should we create an action item to address this concern?" The choice is the group's.

By taking this step, any questions about the intended actions can be answered. Clarifications can be made. The group leaves with a sense of accomplishment and confidence that upcoming action will solve the problem.

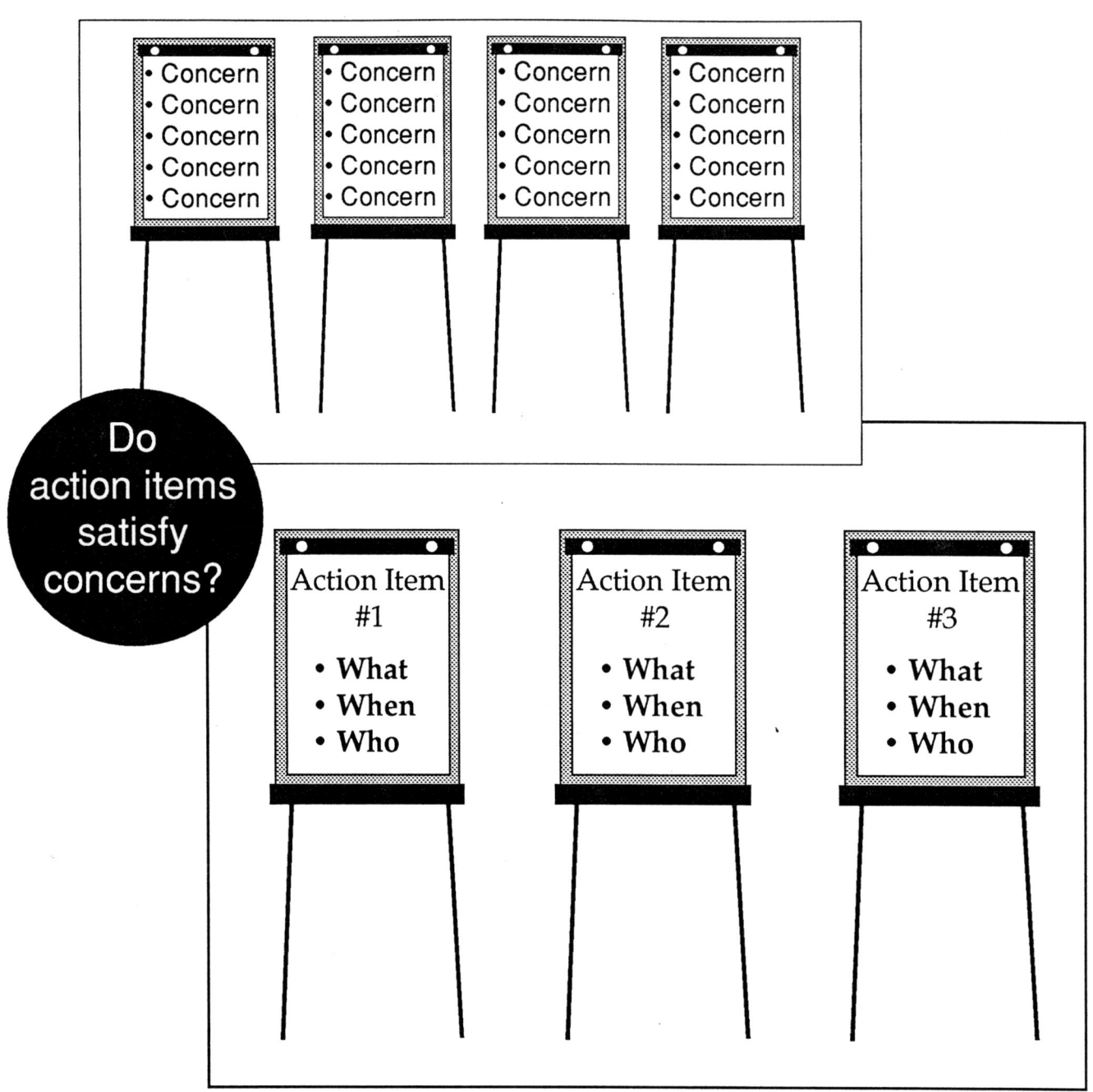

1
Issue?

2 Concerns	Possibilities 3
Action 5	Criteria 4

Check?
6

Doing a "check" at the end...

Why do it?

- It provides closure on the process

- It assures that action items address group concerns

How is it done?

- Display the group's original list of concerns

- Display the group's list of action items

- Start at Concern #1 and ask the group, "Does any of our action items address this concern?"

- If the answer is yes, continue to Concern #2

- If the answer is no, then ask the group, "Should we modify one of our action items or make a new action item to addresss this concern?" *Then do what the group decides.*

- Continue through all concerns on the list in the same manner

Case Study: Shouldn't we do a check?

Background

Three weeks had passed since the team had issued its report. Nine distinct action items were reported to the plant, each with the objective of improving customer service. The team was happy with its work and very proud of the action plan it created for the plant.

However, Doug, an information systems supervisor, was not as satisfied as the team. At the weekly management team meeting, Doug raised his hand and asked, "Why didn't the team include some action on getting feedback from us on these nine items?"

"We talked a lot about getting feedback," Tom answered, "but I guess we neglected to include any specific process in our action items."

"Well that's pretty short sighted," Doug replied. "How can you expect to improve our customer service rating if we don't have any way to get feedback?"

Tom turned to Brenda, sitting next to him, and whispered, "Why didn't the group include something on feedback in their action plan?"

"Because we forgot. I didn't even think about it until now!" Brenda whispered back. "What should we do?"

"Good point, Doug," Tom said turning away from Brenda, "we should have included that concern in our action list. I guess we just made a mistake!"

"Tom, we talked about the importance of feedback during the concerns segment of our meetings," Brenda said quietly, "so why didn't anything on feedback show up in our action items?"

The Problem

The group's action items did not address one of their more important concerns: feedback to plant's management team. And it wasn't until three later that this oversight was discovered.

What Happened?

Tom, as the group's facilitator, neglected to do a final "check" with the group to assure that all concerns had been met through the team's action items.

The Lesson

Most facilitators skip over this step because everyone is eager to wrap-up the meeting and "get back to work." Before adjourning, the facilitator should ask the group, *"Should we check our action items against the group's concerns? Let's be certain that the group's actions satisfy its concerns... would that be OK with everyone?"*

Do the following before disbanding the group:

1 *Review the original list of concerns.* If they are written on flipchart sheets, then tape them on the wall for everyone to see. It written on small sheets, then make copies for each participant.

2 *Check to see if each concern is addressed by one of the action items.* A convenient method is to post the group's list of action items on the wall next to the list of concerns. Let the group study both lists.

3 *Modify or add action items as necessary to cover any action items not addressed.* It is the group's decision whether or not a concern is significant enough to change an existing action item, create a new action item, or do nothing. Many times a group discovers a concern unaddressed by its action plan but may consider it unimportant enough to make any changes to the action item list.

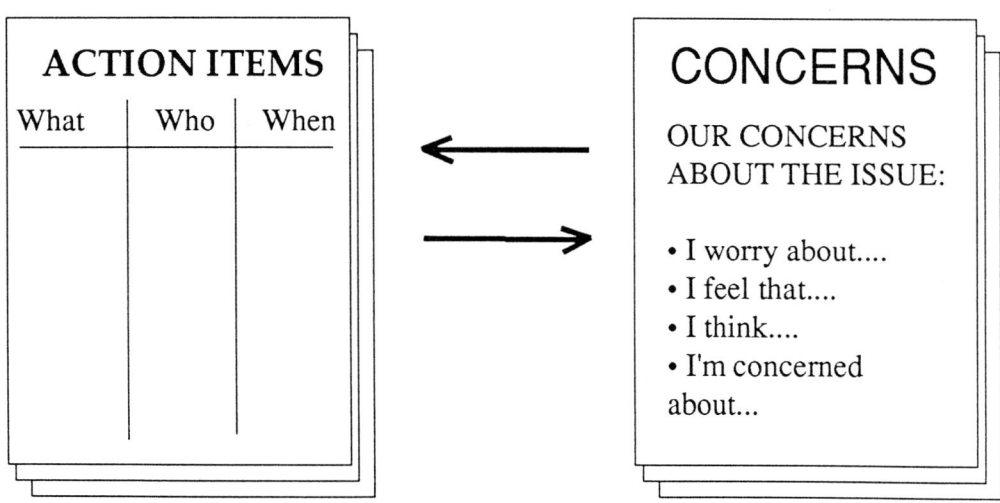

II

Doing It!

7 GETTING STARTED

How do you start?

First, you must **plan ahead**. This means addressing the basics of any meeting:

- **Where** will it held?
- **When** will it held?
- **Who** will attend?
- **What** will be the issue?

These four questions are best answered by discussing them with the leader (see the section "You and the Leader").

Second, you must **notify** the participants.

Third, you must **prepare** your flipcharts.

Fourth, you must **set up** the room.

Then you will be ready to start your facilitation of the group.

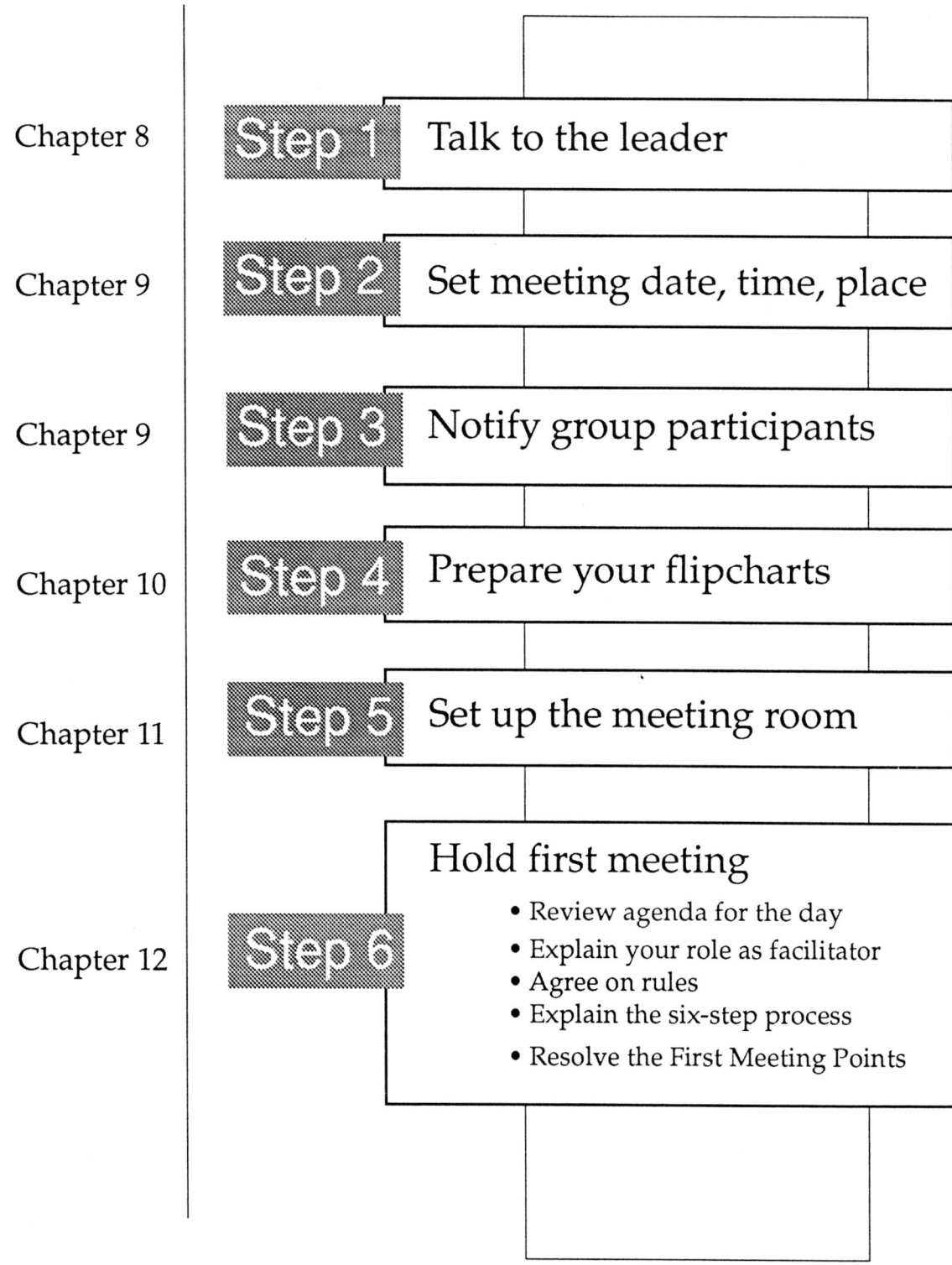

Chapter 8	**Step 1** Talk to the leader
Chapter 9	**Step 2** Set meeting date, time, place
Chapter 9	**Step 3** Notify group participants
Chapter 10	**Step 4** Prepare your flipcharts
Chapter 11	**Step 5** Set up the meeting room
Chapter 12	**Step 6** Hold first meeting

Hold first meeting
- Review agenda for the day
- Explain your role as facilitator
- Agree on rules
- Explain the six-step process
- Resolve the First Meeting Points

Roadmap to the First Meeting

8

YOU AND THE LEADER

We occasionally forget that there is someone else that plays a major role in facilitating a group. That person (or persons) is the leader.

Historically, groups have attempted to make decisions with the leader as the meeting facilitator. It is very natural for a supervisor to call a meeting of her or his direct reports in order to resolve some issue. The difficulties of having such an imbalance of power (and consequences) around the table are obvious.

One of the benefits of facilitated decision-making is that the facilitator is neutral. But there is a very important relationship between the facilitator and the leader. The facilitator will ask the leader for some specific empowerment to manage the process during the meeting. And the leader will expect the facilitator, while remaining neutral to the issue, to achieve some specific results.

This relationship is important and should not be understated as a key relationship during the process.

The leader is someone who has initiated this process by asking for a facilitator (you) to help his or her group address some issue.

It is very important that you as the facilitator and the leader have a clear understanding and agreement regarding (1) the process, (2) the roles/relationships of the group, the facilitator, & leader, and (3) the leader's expectations of this facilitative process.

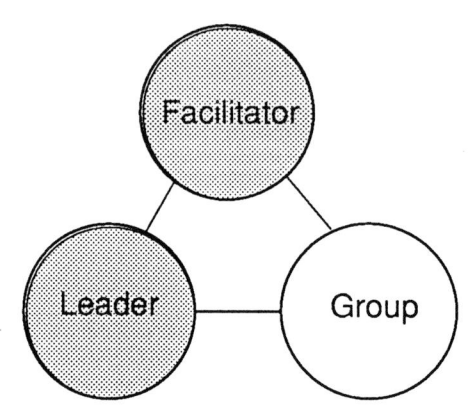

Initial Meeting with the Leader

1 | **Review your role as a facilitator:**
- Neutral
- Facilitator owns the process
- Group owns the content

2 | **Review role of the leader**
- Obeys the rules created by the group
- Acts as member of the group
- Supports the process

3 | **Get agreement from leader on your role as facilitator**

4 | **Determine the following:**
- Issue (leader's viewpoint)
- Time frame for the process
- Group's membership... right people? Others?
- Leader's needs from the group
- Special needs of the group (leader's viewpoint)

5 | **Set time & place for first meeting of the group**

WORKSHEET

Directions: Photocopy this worksheet. Use it during your initial meeting with the leader. Use the information you collect to plan your first meeting with the group.

---

1. Who is the leader(s)?

2. What is the leader's objective in working a facilitative process with the group?

3. What is the leader's idea of the "issue statement" for the group?

4. Some key elements or points that the leader would like covered as part of the process...

5. Time frame?
- Start:

- End process:

- "drop-dead" deadline:

6. Members of the group...

7. Other people that maybe should be part of the group...

8. Special needs of the leader....

9. Special needs of the group...

10. Leader's opinion on:
- Meeting frequency

- Meeting location

- Meeting day & time

"No one gets credit for being prepared... they only get credit for getting results."

- **Old Saying**

PRE-MEETING LOGISTICS

Before you move ahead, do three things:

- First, you must **set the date, time, & place** of the meeting.

- Second, you must **reserve the room**.

- Third, you must **notify** the participants.

The first two items can be directly accomplished. The third, notifying the participants, should follow the format shown in the following example.

In addition to these logistical items, two other tasks must be done: preparing your flipcharts and setting up the meeting room. Chapters 10 & 11 address each subject, respectively.

Let's look at an example of how to notify the participants of the upcoming group facilitation...

Example of pre-meeting "Welcome Letter"

• **Identify the leader(or sponsor) of this activity.**

    • **What are the benefits of doing this?**

• **When & where?**

    • **Identify any pre- work.**

• **Questions?**

• **Positive reinforcement for participating!**

MEMORANDUM

Salt Lake City, UT
November 24

Night Crew -
Group Facilitation

Caroline,
Our supervisor, Suzie, has asked that your work team **solve a problem** regarding cost accounting of damaged merchandise. She has **asked me to facilitate** a seried of problem-solving meetings with the night crew.

The **benefits** of solving this problem are:
    • lower operating costs
    • fewer injuries
    • increased break time for crew members

We will hold **our first meeting** at 10:00 a.m. on this coming December 26 in the company conference room.

Before the meeting, please review the attached company policy on damaged merchandise and **be prepared to brainstorm possible solutions**. I will be a neutral facilitator during these meetings and my goal is to help the group identify needed action items to solve this problem.

Please call me at 123-4567 if I can answer any questions regarding the meeting objectives or the facilitation process.

Thank you for helping the night crew solve this problem!

Danielle

attachments
cc: Suzie

Importance of the Welcome Letter

> "Man is a tool-using animal... Without tools he is nothing, with tools he is all."
>
> — Thomas Carlyle

10 FLIPCHARTS AND TOOLS

You as the facilitator work using *visual devices*.

Human beings are visual animals and function better when ideas and concepts are graphically represented for them. And since you own the process, you will need to use the appropriate tools to maintain a *visual format* for the group.

With experience you will repeatedly depend on same tools: flipcharts, pens, Post-It™ notes, masking tape. If you conduct formal facilitations long enough, you probably will assemble a *toolkit* containing these items (expect the flipcharts) for your convenience.

Most successful facilitators routinely prepare their flipcharts, wallcharts, and other visual aids beforehand. Learning to select and use the correct tools will not only save you time, but will also enhance the group's perception of your facilitation skills.

Facilitator's Toolkit

- Tape, 3/4" transparent
- Tape, masking, 1" wide
- Tape, white, correction type, 1" wide
- Dots, adhesive, 3/4" diameter, colored
- Scissors
- Marking Pens, chisel (broad) point
- 3M Post-It™ notes
- Ruler, 18"
- Paper clips
- Pencil (preferrably blue)
- Flipchart easel
- Flipchart pads (1" square grids)
- Watch or clock
- Smile, big one

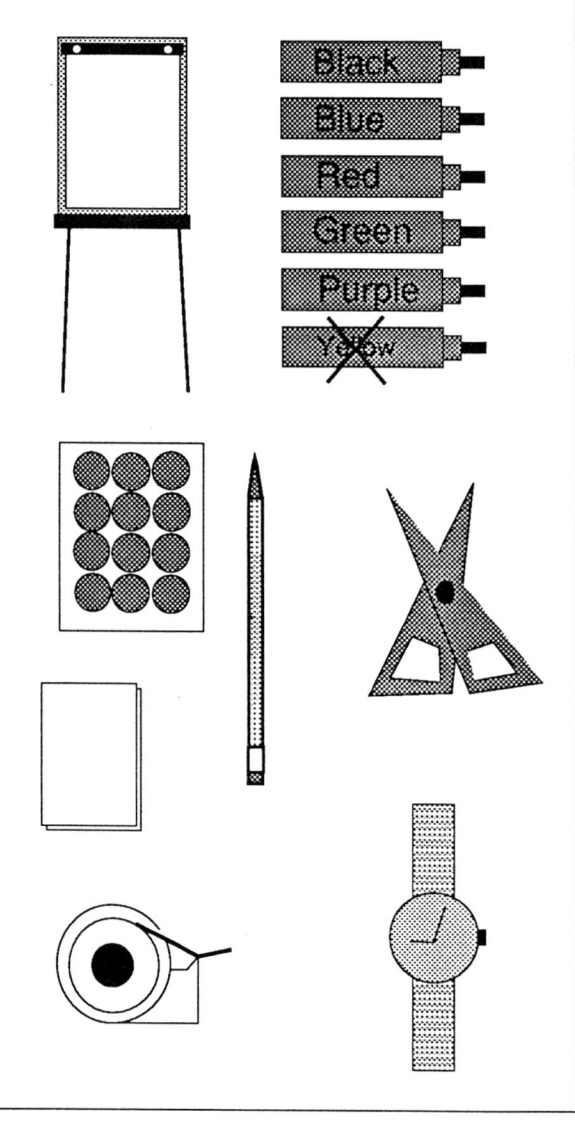

TIP Your large pens should be a water-base type and not the solvent or alcohol-base type. Why? Because the solvent pens bleed through the paper and mark the next flipchart. And the smell really gets to you after writing with them!

TIP Make a mistake while writing on the flipchart? Just use the 1" white correction tape and cover it up! It's neat and you can just write directly on the tape... and the group won't be able to tell the difference!

—I CARRY MY TOOLS IN A SPECIAL BAG!

COLORS !!

How boring is the repetitive use of a black pen on a white flipchart! Often we forget that people like colors. Drab, monotonous black marker pens are too common in facilitation sessions! Why not add some spice to your session use some colors?

Research has shown that different colors create different responses in people. Let's look at some colors and their effect on people.

Blue is the most favorite color. Blue relaxes people. The absence of red makes it less tiring than the warmer violet. More importantly, blue sparks creativity in people. *Use blue backgrounds or blue lettering in your flipcharts when collecting concerns or brainstorming.* Never use blue when writing warning or cautionary statements.

Violet, the reddish sister of blue, is the most restful color. Violet creates the aura of power and self-confidence. Whereas blue triggers creativity in people, violet is more relaxing. Clinical research shows that it reduces blood pressure, pulse and respiration rates. But be careful! Large solid blocks of violet can be overwhelming so use it only for lettering and not as backgrounds in large areas.

Red is the most stimulating color. Red increases blood pressure, pulse and respiration rates. Red is the color to use when an exclamatory title is needed on a flipchart. Cautions, warnings, and other "participant-beware" statements should be written in large, red letters. *Warning: writing in red can be hard to see for most people, so always use letters at least three inches tall when using a red marker pen.* Interestingly enough, splashes of red can enhance creativity and the appetite of a group.

Orange, red's yellowish brother, is an exciting color. It raises your heart rate but lacks the punch of red. Because of this it is called a "cheap" color. Orange should be avoided as a color for lettering unless it is used sparingly and with very tall letters. Why? Orange is difficult to see. It lacks red's importance. If you want to deliver the message of importance then write in red! The best use for orange on flipcharts is as a border or a highlight.

Yellow is brightest and most cheerful color. It is never to be used alone for lettering unless you want to punish your group (you can't see yellow on white paper!). Yellow can raise the frustration level of a group when the color is used in large amounts. The best use for yellow is as a highlight on your flipcharts.

Green, is the an unsettling color. It lives between cheerful yellow and relaxing blue, creating a degree of uneasiness in the viewer. Green can inspire both excitement and passiveness. This schizophrenic nature suggests that it be used sparingly on flipcharts. This might seem a drastic step, especially since most of nature is colored green, but a prudent one when facilitating groups. Green is best used for borders and accents.

Be careful when using several colors on a single flipchart page. Limit yourself to *three colors* plus black.

Color	Impact on Group	Best Use on Flipchart
Blue	Creativity	• Text Lettering • Backgrounds
Violet	Restfulness	• Lettering
Red	Stimulation	• Warnings/Notices • Borders • Highlights • Accents
Orange	Excitement	• Border • Highlights
Yellow	Cheerful	• High lights
Green	Unsettling	• Borders • Accents

YOU WANT TO COME TO OUR FACILITATION SESSION? WE NEED THE COLOR!

Flipchart Management

(A) USE 2 OR MORE FLIPCHART EASELS...

(B) WHEN TURNING PAGES, <u>ROLL</u> THE SHEET OVER...

—I GRAB THE LOWER CORNER OF THE PAGE!

(C) TO TEAR OFF A SHEET, FIRST RIP ½" ALONG PERFORATION AND THEN PULL DOWN AT AN ANGLE...

> "The proof of the pudding is in the eating."
> **- Miguel de Cervantes**
> from *Don Quixote de la Mancha*

11 THE ROOM

Two hours is the optimal time for a facilitated, problem-solving meeting.

During those two hours, participants will remain in a room that can either help or hurt the process. Your responsibility as a facilitator is to prepare the room so that it conveys a positive atmosphere to the proceeding.

This is one of the most frequently overlooked steps in a successful facilitation. Here are some suggestions on how to make the room help you... and also help the group be more effective during their problem-solving meeting.

Warning: Always take the time (about 30 minutes) before the meeting to arrange the room. Plan to come early and leave late at every facilitation you undertake.

How the room looks to the group...

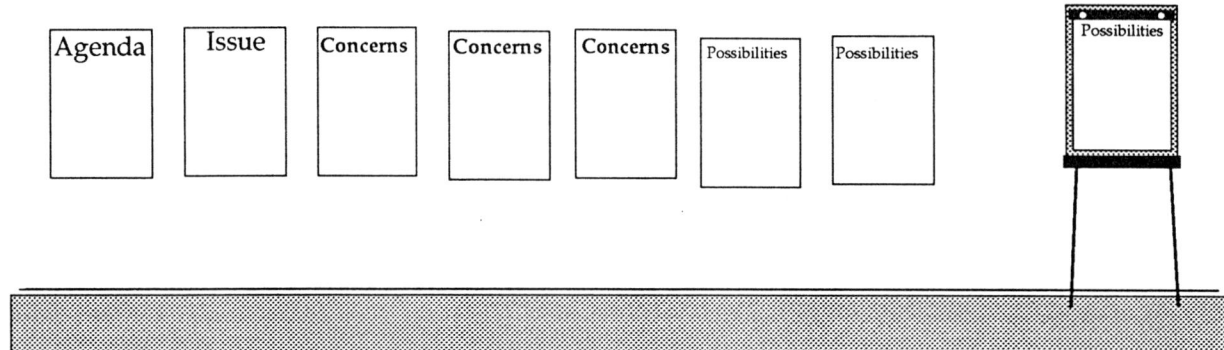

SUGGESTIONS:

- Stand in front of group
- Use a flipchart easel
- Hang flipchart sheets in front of group
- The more bright lighting the better!

How the room looks from overhead...

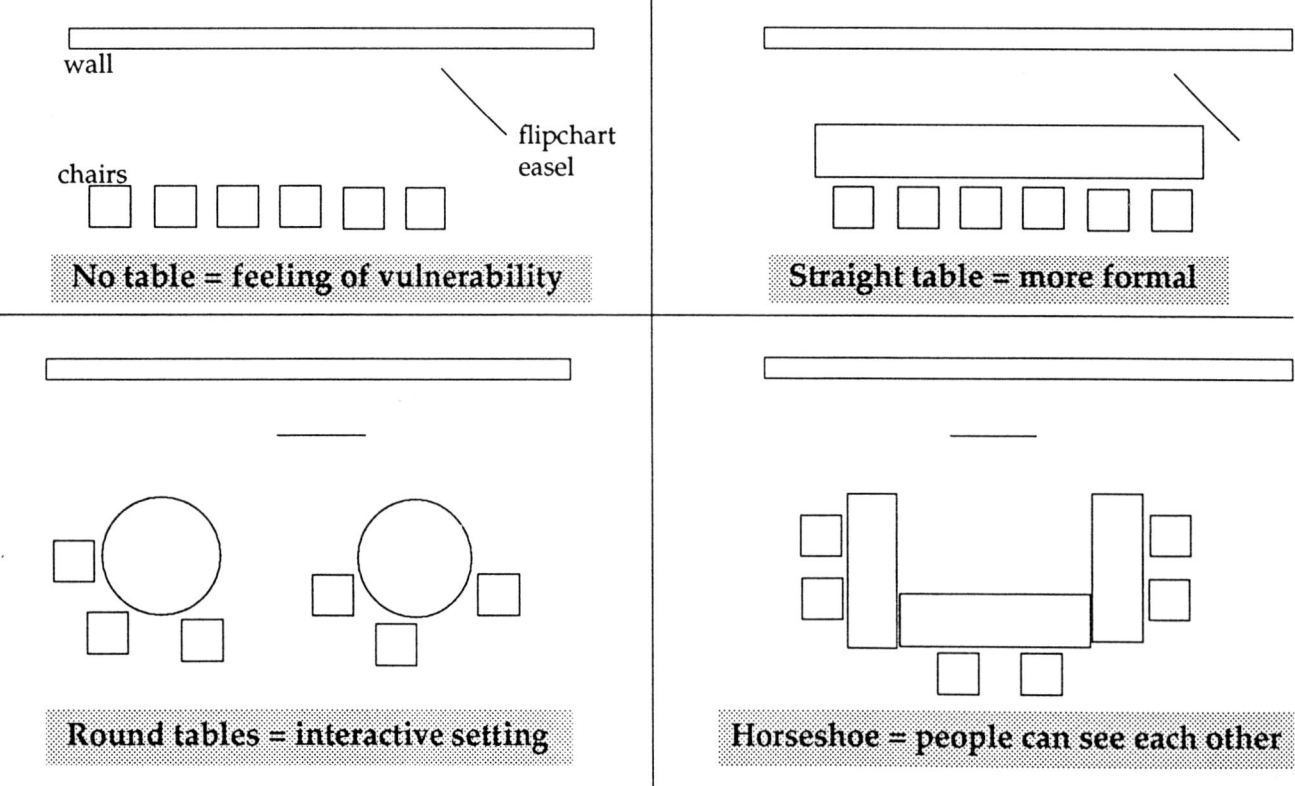

Suggested room setup...

12 THE FIRST MEETING

The day has arrived for your first group meeting. Ready to go?

There are five steps to follow in the *first* meeting:
- #1 - Review the agenda
- #2 - Explain your role
- #3 - Agree on rules of conduct
- #4 - Explain the six-step problem-solving process
- #5 - Resolve some important issues called "The First Meeting Points"

Schedule the meeting for two hours. After two hours, stop. You'll need a break... and the group will need time to think over the issues and materials reviewed.

And don't forget to schedule the *second* meeting before everyone leaves the meeting room!

Hold first meeting

Step 1

- Review agenda for the day
- Explain your role as facilitator
- Agree on rules
- Explain the six-step process
- Resolve the First Meeting Points

- Make the agenda *before* the meeting

- Review the agenda (aloud) with the group

- Ask the group, "Is there anything you want to add or change?" (If so... do it!)

- Finish by asking the group, "What time do we want to finish today?"

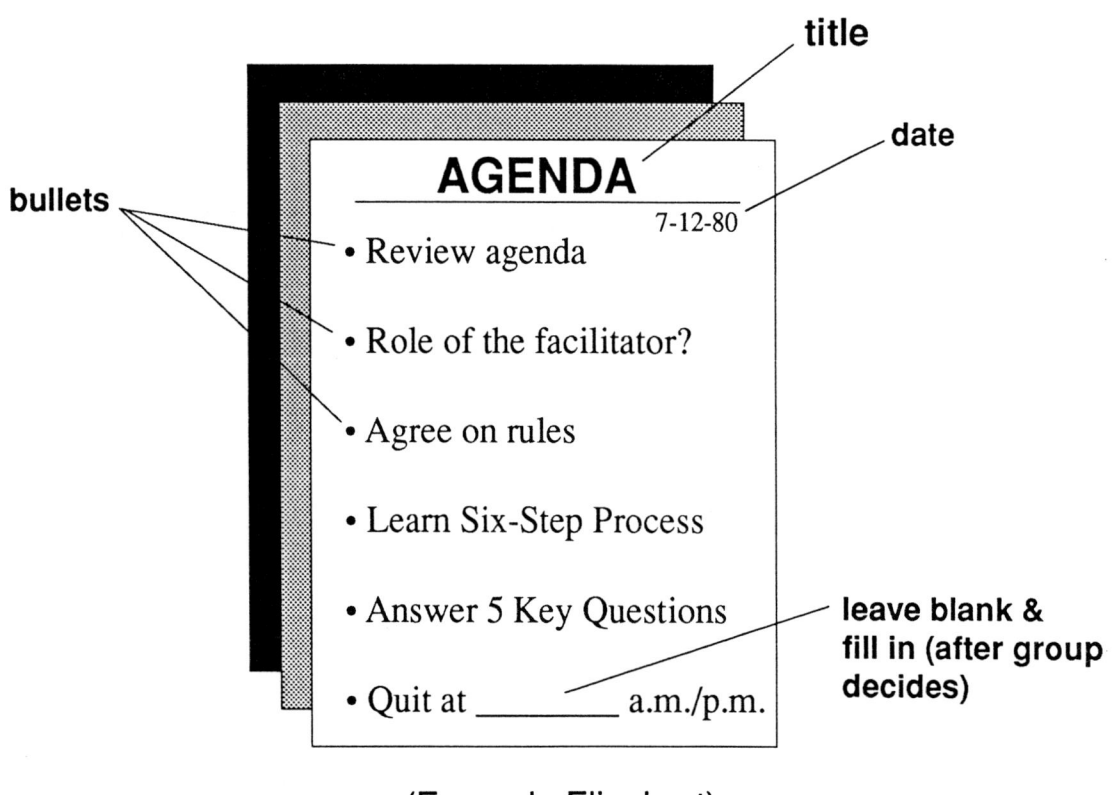

title

date

bullets

AGENDA

7-12-80

- Review agenda

- Role of the facilitator?

- Agree on rules

- Learn Six-Step Process

- Answer 5 Key Questions

- Quit at _____ a.m./p.m.

leave blank & fill in (after group decides)

(Example Flipchart)

Hold first meeting

Step 2

- Review agenda for the day
- Explain your role as facilitator
- Agree on rules
- Explain the six-step process
- Resolve the First Meeting Points

Share with the group some thoughts about your role...

- "...I'm here to *help* the group!"
- "...I'm *neutral* on this issue!"
- "...please help me... if your see me not being neutral, please *stop me* and tell me!"
- "...the group owns the *content* and I own the *process* we'll follow in this meeting."
- "...my job is to *enforce* the process and the rules."

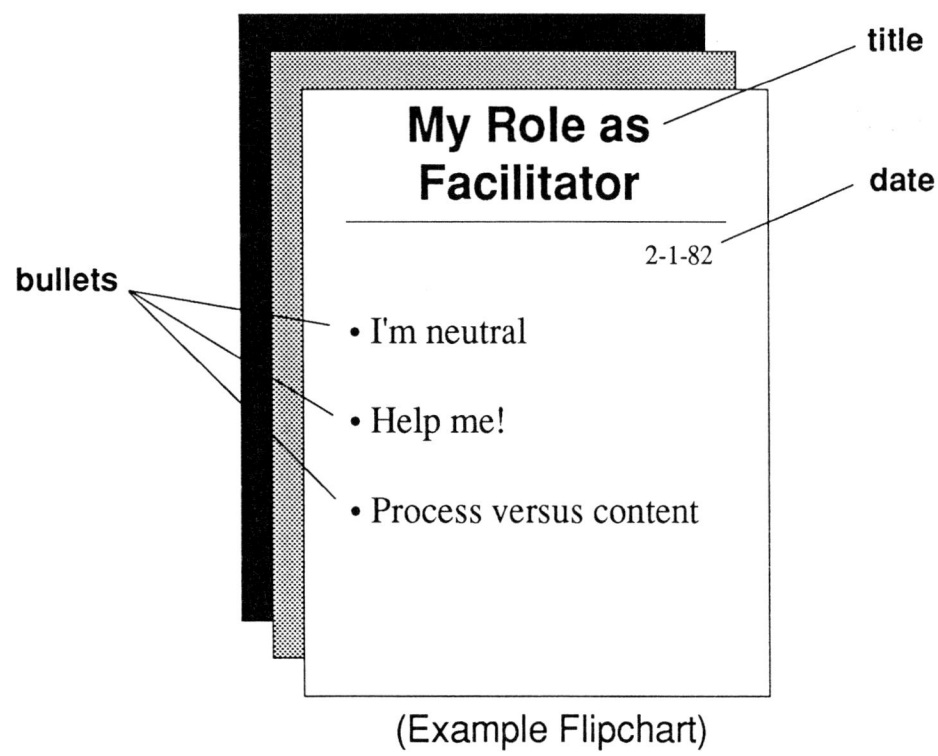

title

My Role as Facilitator

date

2-1-82

bullets

- I'm neutral

- Help me!

- Process versus content

(Example Flipchart)

12-3

Hold first meeting
Step 3
- Review agenda for the day
- Explain your role as facilitator
- Agree on rules
- Explain the six-step process
- Resolve the First Meeting Points

- Make a flipchart of rules

- Hang flipchart on wall in meeting room

- Ask the group, "Do you agree with these rules?"

- Delete, add, or change the rules as the group desires

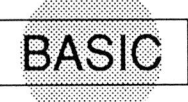

Rules for the Group

❋ Only one person speaks at a time

❋ No side conversations

❋ Silence is acceptable

❋ No rank in the room

❋ Everyone participates

❋ No one dominates

❋ What is said stays in the room

❋ This is a "safe zone" to speak in

❋ No "grand-standing"

❋ Attack problems, not people

❋ Group will follow the process

❋ OK to question the process at any time

❋ OK to change the rules

❋ OK to change the process

❋ OK to change your mind

❋ Facilitator will enforce the rules

❋ Group will help the facilitator

❋ End on time

• Make these rules on a separate flipchart

• Ask the group, "Would you like to include any of these rules, also?"

Hold first meeting
• Review agenda for the day
• Explain your role as facilitator
 • Agree on rules
• Explain the six-step process
• Resolve the First Meeting Points

ADVANCED

More Rules for the Group

✳ No negative responses from other group members for someone raising an issue at any time

✳ Group focuses on "true consensus" versus "driving to completion"

✳ Members don't respond defensively to questions

✳ Members use tact - questions are asked supportively for understanding versus asked aggressively

✳ Listen as an ally

✳ Give freely of your experience

✳ Keep an open mind

✳ Be an active lister

Hold first meeting
- Review agenda for the day
- Explain your role as facilitator
- Agree on rules
- Explain the six-step process
- Resolve the First Meeting Points

• Make a flipchart

• Hang flipchart on wall in
      meeting room

See the section "Introduction" for
more information regarding the six
steps of the facilitation process.

❶
Issue?

❷ Concerns	Possibilities ❸
Action ❺	Criteria ❹

Check?
❻

(Example Flipchart)

Hold first meeting

- Review agenda for the day
- Explain your role as facilitator
- Agree on rules
- Explain the six-step process
- Resolve the First Meeting Points

At the *first* meeting, the facilitator and the group need to have an open discussion about the process. **Don't get trapped by talking about content items.** Talk about the process the group will follow to achieve resolution of the issue at hand.

A good way to come to some agreement with the group over the process steps is to discuss the five sets of questions below.

During the first meeting, help the group resolve these five points...

1

What is the scope of the task?
What is the purpose of the group? What are the problems/issues? Are there any limitations of the group? Boundaries?

2

Authority level?
What authority does the group possess? Gather information? Recommend action? Make decisions? Implement action?

3

Success looks like...
What is the goal? What will the final product look like?

4

What process will be used?
Who are the stakeholders? How will decisions be made within the group? Consensus-based? How will the group communicate with other individuals or groups?

5

Timing?
What is expected by when?

WARNING

Stakeholders: individuals that are...

- **responsible for final decisions**
  or
- **affected by those decisions**
  or
- **have power to block those decisions**

• This is a very important issue to resolve at the *first* meeting. (See Question #4, "What Process Will Be Used?" on the previous page)

• Stakeholders can undo any progress made by the team. Recommendations can be *ignored* by stakeholders. Decisions can be *reversed* by them. Actions can be *cancelled* by them.

• A solution to the problem of stakeholders is to *include them* in the process. If that is not possible, then the group must implement and use some kind of *communication link* with them. Such communication will keep the stakeholders abreast of group actions and decisions... and avoid unpleasant surprises to either group.

What are stakeholders?

Review

The First Meeting

- Review agenda for the day

- Explain your role as facilitator

- Agree on rules

- Explain the six-step process

- Resolve the First Meeting Points

And remember...

- Schedule the meeting for two hours

- Schedule the *second* meeting before everyone leaves the meeting room!

13 BUILDING CONSENSUS

Consensus is the means by which groups agree on which possibilities "survive" to become action items. It is a useful tool that enables the group to avoid hopeless deadlocks and move ahead in the process. Conventional voting to determine agreement should be discouraged by the facilitator because it forces individuals to entrench themselves in positions they later hesitate to change.

The following pages provide several methods for you as a facilitator to help a group reach consensus. Remember, consensus doesn't mean that everyone in the group <u>agrees</u> with the decision... it only means that they will <u>support</u> it.

Consensus

"Consensus is reached when everyone in the group can buy into, or live with, the decision without feeling compromised in any way."

-Michael Doyle & David Straus

"You may not agree completely with the decision, but you'll openly support it."

- Gregory Putz

Benefits of Consensus

Decisions are more accurate
People are more willing to support decisions
Disagreements are explored rather than avoided
Everyone gets a chance to be heard
Everyone ends up with more information
Group synergism creates a higher-quality decision

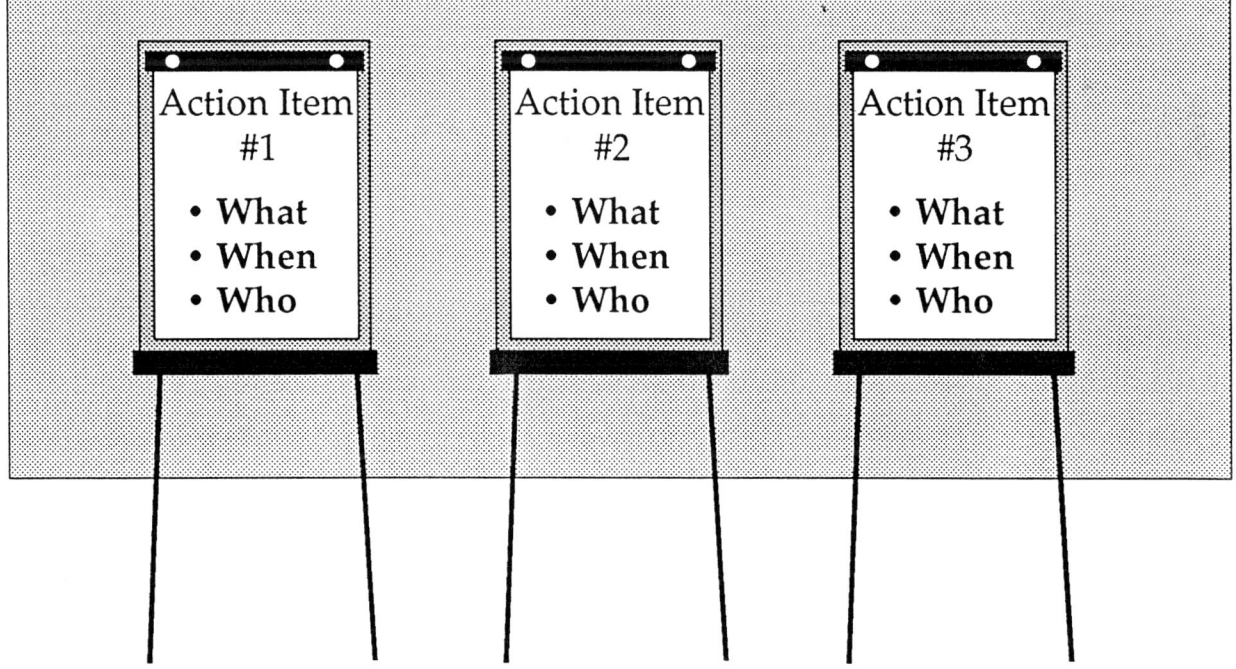

Guidelines for Reaching Consensus

For each individual

✳ Don't argue for your personal judgements but approach from a standpoint of logic.

✳ Don't change your mind just to avoid conflict and reach a speedy agreement. Look for a common ground of solutions that may not be precisely what you think right but close enough.

✳ Always remember that conflict, differences of opinion and interpretation are a helpful, strengthening attribute of consensus-building.

DON'T VOTE!

Why not vote?
• **Voting causes an individual to establish a position... and it is difficult for anyone to publicly change his or her position**

• **Voting ignores the opinions of the minority**

• **Voting avoids conflict and discussion... it denies the group the benefit of understanding others and the natural synergism created by group interaction**

As the facilitator

◆ Make absolutely clear to the group what it is that they are seeking consensus on.

◆ Start off by getting the group to agree to some "lofty" or superordinate goal... a noble objective that they all will strive for in attempting to build a consensus.

◆ A certain amount of tension in the room is expected and helpful. Don't initiate any activity that prematurely smooths-over the conflict.

◆ Avoid any technique that reduces conflict, such as trading, voting, numerical averaging, coin-flips, or bargaining.

◆ Require that each individual take responsibility for hearing others and being heard... everyone participates actively and is included in building the consensus.

◆ Keep insisting that there be a "win/win" environment in the room. A win by the group and the individuals are more important than an solitary, individual win.

◆ Remind the group that conflict is good in creating consensus and is not a hinderance to it. Differences of opinion and disagreement are natural and expected.

DON'T VOTE!

Building Consensus

Tool Box

Negative Voting	Ask, "Can anyone <u>not</u> live with this proposal?" Ask, "Does anyone have any heartache with this...?"
Straw Voting	Say, "OK, I just want to get a feel for where we are... this is a non-binding straw vote. How many of you can support this...?"
Win/Win	Say, "OK, it seems that you cannot support this part of the proposal... what would we have to change to make it acceptable to you?"

Hey ! Are you on the road to building some consensus with your group? If so, then try this little tool called...

FIST or FIVE ??

Step ① Annouce the *Fist or Five* process by say, "I want to get a feel for where the group stands on this topic. Let's take an informal, straw vote that's not binding on anyone."

Step ② Clarify the *Fist or Five* process by explaining, "After I ask the question, I'd like everyone to indicate their current feeling about this by raising their hand with their fingers as such:

 **Five Fingers =** YES! I agree. No more discussion! Let's move on...

 **Four Fingers =** OK with me. I can support the group on this topic.

 **Three Fingers =** I'm on the fence. Can we continue talking about it?

 **Two Fingers =** I *really* don't know. I really need to talk about this a lot more.

 One Finger = No. I really can't support this. We can talk, but you'll really have to convince me!

 No Fingers = HECK, NO !! No way. No how. Forget it !!

Step ③ Vote and determine the average. If the average number of fingers is one, then say, "OK. The result is overwhelmingly a "one" so let's continue talking..." If the average is five, say "OK, everyone seems to support this topic, so let's move on to something else."

Building Consensus

Summary

• Complete unanimity is NOT the goal.

• Discourage those who ARGUE for their position.

• Do not let the group assume that it is a win-lose situation. Encourage a WIN-WIN arrangement.

• Discourage those who change their mind simply to AVOID conflict.

• Guide the group so as to AVOID conflict-reducing techniques like voting, averaging, coin-tosses, etc.

• Be realistic - differences of opinion within the group are HEALTHY and natural; they frequently result in synergism helpful to the process.

• Do not become discouraged at the TIME REQUIRED to reach consensus; if the group becomes weary then take a break or schedule another meeting.

14 HANDLING CONFLICT

Conflict is natural. It creates both benefits and detriments to the group. Its beneficial nature includes diversity of thought, group synergy, and personal enthusiasm. Its drawbacks are wasted time, animosity, and emotional roadblocks.

As a facilitator, you must learn how to recognize the types of conflicts and how to mitigate them. Interventions range from subtle to dramatic. Each has its place in facilitition sessions.

Your role as facilitator is to harness the group's energy and allow the natural synergism to produce its invaluable ideas.

The following pages provide the necessary information for dealing with conflict and directing it to benefit the process.

Group Dynamics

- The late comer...
- The early leaver...
- The broken record...
- The Doubting Thomas...
- The head shaker...
- The dropout...
- The whisperer...
- The loud mouth...
- The attacker...
- The interpreter...
- The gossiper...
- The know-it-all...
- The back seat driver...
- The busy body...
- The interrupter...
- The teacher's pet...

Handling CONFRONTATION in meetings...

STEP **1**   Clarify objectives

STEP **2**   Strive for understanding

STEP **3**   Focus on the rationale

STEP **4**   Generate alternatives

STEP **5**   Allow for "soak time" and take a break

STEP **6**   Use humor

Common Approaches to Conflict

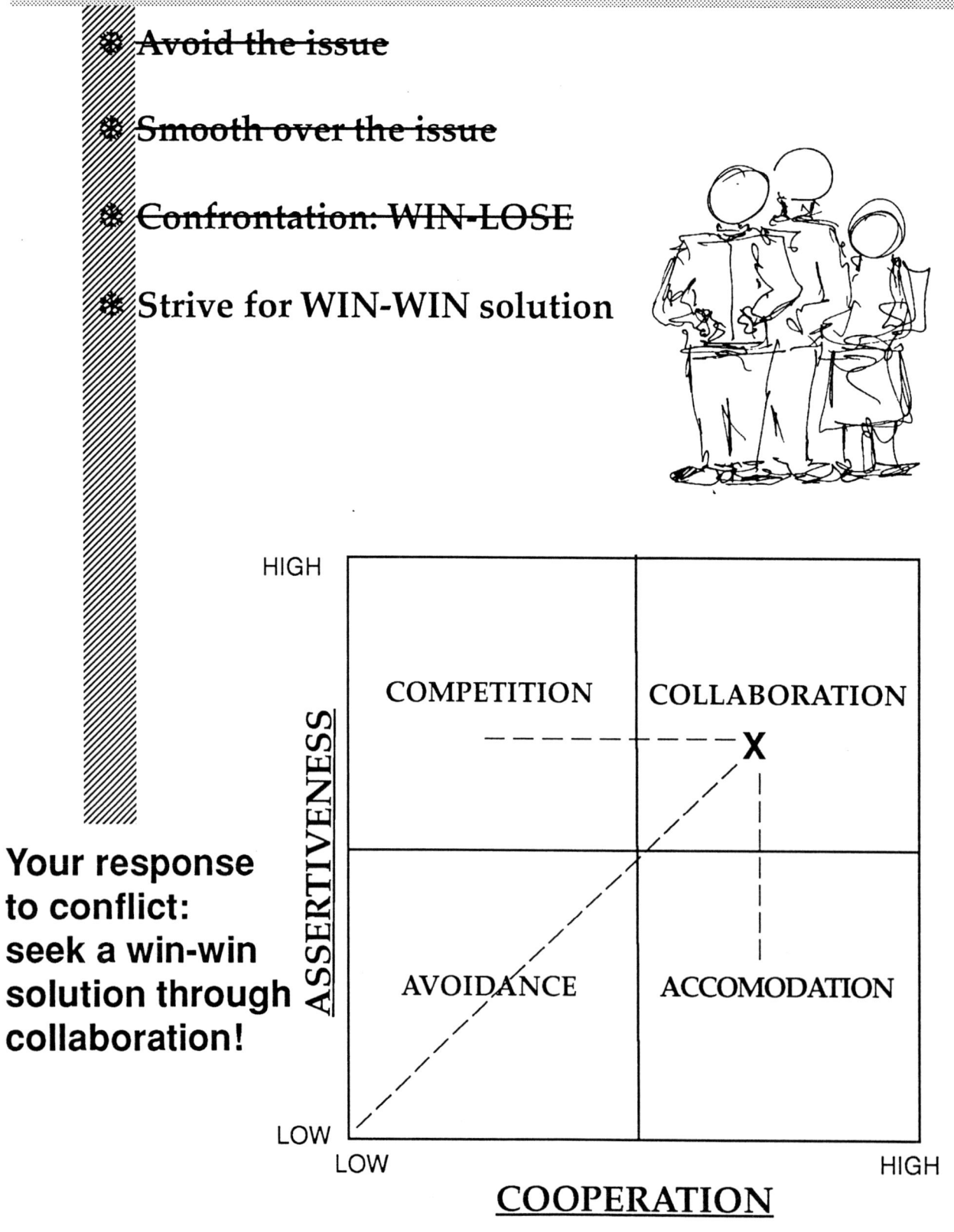

* ~~Avoid the issue~~

* ~~Smooth over the issue~~

* ~~Confrontation: WIN-LOSE~~

* Strive for WIN-WIN solution

Your response to conflict: seek a win-win solution through collaboration!

INTERVENTIONS

IGNORE

PAUSE (be quiet)

PAUSE & LOOK (at the person)

PAUSE & ASK A QUESTION
(to the person: "Hey, Bob, what
do you think about this?")

WALK OVER TO THE PERSON
(and stand nearby)

TOUCH PERSON (lightly...
while you continue to talk)

TELL THE GROUP, "LET'S
TAKE A BREAK NOW"

TAKE A BREAK & CONFRONT
THE PERSON (privately)

CONFRONT THE PERSON
DURING THE MEETING

By the Facilitator

III

Appendices

> "If A equals success, then the formula is A equals X plus Y plus Z. X is work. Y is play. Z is keep your mouth shut."
> — **Albert Einstein**

15
DO'S & DON'TS

Now that you have had an opportunity to learn the process steps of being a facilitator, it's time to learn some lessons from experienced facilitators.

Each facilitation session is unique. There are, however, a number of rules that help you avoid catastrophy. If you follow these do's and don'ts, then you will be successful as a neutral facilitator.

I guarantee it.

Do

- **Meet with the leader** before the group-facilitation session
- Be **early** to the group sesson
- Have the **room set-up** and **flipcharts prepared** beforehand
- Have a **plan** for the process steps you will follow
- Have a **back-up plan** if you get stuck in the process
- **Listen** to the needs & wants of the group
- Be **flexible** with the group
- Be **firm**
- Use **humor**
- Be **postive** & up-beat
- **End on-time** each group-facilitation session

Don't

- Don't argue
- Don't get angry
- Don't threaten the group
- Don't tolerate personal attacks upon anyone
- Don't let the group discussion get too far off the subject
- Don't write on flipcharts with a yellow-colored pen
- Don't be afraid to ask "What would the group like to do with that?"
- Don't forget that you are NEUTRAL... and remain so until you tell the group that you are "taking off your facilitator's hat" to give your personal opinion on the subject... otherwise, keep your opinions to yourself!
- Don't be late

Helpful Hints

• When you're in front of the group as the facilitator, it's OK to **be entertaining** because, as they say in show business, "entertainment is the spice of life!" And people love to be entertained! Hemerrhoidal behavior is *not* a necessary trait for any facilitator's success.

• Use lots of **colors** in diagrams & drawings... why? Because people like color!

• Keep things **moving quickly**... forge ahead and keep going. If you don't, people will get bored and disengage themselves from the process.

• Always be **one step ahead** of the group (example: have the next flipchart sheet ready to use for the next topic or process step).

• Always **listen**. And if you cannot, don't try to fake it! Instead, say "I'm sorry, but I didn't catch what you just said..."

• Keep **focused** that you are there to **get a job done**. You are not being paid by the flipchart page completed... so help the group overcome wasteful tangents, arguments, or roadblocks.

• Don't be scared to occassionally **"let out the leash"** when the group's discussion ventures into new territory... it may pay dividends with new ideas or the a better understanding of the topic by some members.

• If you get stuck and don't know what to say, then just tell the group **"Let's take a break!"**

16

FREQUENTLY-ASKED QUESTIONS

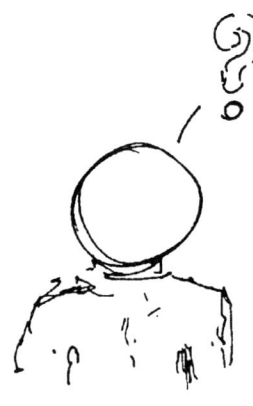

Here are answers to questions frequently asked about facilitation:

Question #1
"I've been asked to facilitate a group next week. The group is not my work group but they work in the same building. I've never done this before. What should I do to get started?"

<u>Answer</u>
Your first task is to study the process steps in facilitation (issue, concerns, possibilities, criteria, action, check) in <u>Part I</u>.

The second step is to meet with the group's leader before the facilitation session. Cover the checklist in <u>Chapter 8</u>, "You and the Leader."

The third step is the pre-meeting logistics: arrange the first meeting, reserve the room, notify the meeting participants, prepare your flipcharts & visual aids. See the balance of <u>Part II</u>, "Doing It!" for detailed information.

Question #2
"My boss says that she will facilitate an upcoming meeting with our work group. I'm concerned about her remaining an effective facilitator. What do you think?"

Answer
Your concern is a valid one.

It is very, very hard to be a group leader and a neutral facilitator at the same time. Despite her best effort and sincere actions to remain neutral, the group might have some lingering suspicion that she has a hidden agenda.

It is best to find someone outside the group who has no interest in the outcome. That way, the group is more likely to open up and express its true feelings... and the leader can relax and participate in the process without the pressure of managing the process. Remember, the prime objectives are building trust in the process and maximizing group participation. If your boss cannot accomplish these objectives, then find someone who can!

Question #3
"I write like a third grader. If I have to record group comments and ideas on a flipcharts, then I'll be so nervous that I won't be able to manage the process! What should I do?"

Answer
Simple. Recruit someone who has good handwriting to help you.

Having a scribe assist the facilitator is not unusual. In fact, it frees the facilitator to focus more on what is being said by the participants. Plus, it expands group involvement. If you cannot pursuade someone to do it for the entire meeting, then split the writing responsibilities among several people in the group.

You will be pleasantly surprized how many people will gladly assist you in this area!

Question #4
"My work group has had several experiences where their recommendations have been shot down by people outside the group after a series of facilitated meetings. It's almost hopeless now. Nobody wants to spend the time creating action items because someone is always ready to pounce on us afterwards. Any suggestions?"

Answer
This is very common. People that ambush your ideas and actions are known as "duck hunters" or "reed people" because, like hunters, they typically wait in the reeds, pop up, and start "blasting away" at your ideas.

The trick to success is to include these people in your decision-making process.

By virtue of their desire to shoot down your ideas, they must be stakeholders in the output of your group. It is very important to identify these people at your first meeting. The questions to ask the group are, "Who else should be involved in this process? Who out there has some vested interest in what this group decides? Who is going to give us any damaging flak over our actions?"

Question #5
"I've volunteered to facilitate a meeting with my group. Before I send out the meeting announcement, shouldn't I tell them how long the session will last?"

Answer
Good idea. Experience has taught me two things about groups and meeting length: (1) at one hour, a group is just getting warmed-up and participation starts to "take off," and (2) at two hours, a group is typically tired and their energy level is low.

Recommendation? *Schedule the meeting to end after two hours.* If, after two hours, they want to continue then keep going! Just ask every thirty minutes thereafter if they want to continue... it's up to them.

Question #6

"During last week's meeting I facilitated, the group kept asking me for my ideas of what they should do. They wanted my suggestions for solutions to the problem. What should I say?"

Answer

Remember, you are a *neutral* facilitator! You control the process and the group owns the content.

When a group asks you for input on a solution, they're asking you to be involved in the content. If you want to remain neutral you cannot get involved. It's tempting... but don't do it! *Resist the urge to be brilliant!*

What should you do? First, remind the group that you are a neutral facilitator and cannot answer content-oriented questions. Second, "reflect" the question back to the group by asking them, "What do *others* in the group think...?"

If you feel very, very strongly about giving some input and are willing to risk your neutral position, see Question #7 below.

Question #7

"I feel very strongly about the issue being worked by the group. I want to stay a neutral facilitator but I feel that I must speak out! What should I do?"

Answer

OK, this situation occurs to every facilitator.

You may be a expert on the issue. You may have intimate knowledge of the subject. Or you might have some new data about the topic. In any case, you have a burning feeling deep inside you that says, "Tell the group!" *And you sincerely believe that what you will say about the content will help the group solve its problem.*

Here's what you do. First, say, "I'm going to take off my neutral facilitator's hat for a minute." Second, walk from the front of the group to the rear of the room and say what you must. Finally, when finished, return to the front of the group and say, "I'm now putting my neutral facilitator's hat back on." *Warning: do not over do this! Usually, once a meeting at the most!*

Question #8

"Do I have to prepare my flipcharts before the meeting? Why can't I just make them as I go? "

Answer

If it's an informal, spur-of-the-moment problem solving meeting, you can.

But, if it's a future meeting, informal or not, it's always best to prepare the flipcharts ahead of time. Why? Three reasons:

First, it saves you the embarassment of forgetting the next step. *With prepared flipcharts, simply flip the page over and there's the next step!* (Hey, with all the discussion and talk, it's easy to forget what you're doing next!)

Second, the pause and quiet in the room while you prepare the blank flipchart is an interruption to the process flow. It creates opportunities for off-track discussions while you are writing. *If your flipcharts are prepared then you can move along from step to step without hesitation!*

Third, you will create the illusion of an expert facilitator who cares by being prepared! A group will *also* think, "Hey! If she takes the time to prepare those flipcharts, then this must be important stuff!"

Question #9

"When I facilitate my group, there are always side conversations going on in the room. It's distracting to the process! How do I stop people from talking on the side like this? "

Answer

First Step: When you hear the sidebar discussion... stop talking. Your silence will be noticed and the sidebar should end.

Step Two: If the first step does not work, then you should continue talking while slowly walk over to the individuals who are talking and stand near them. Your physical presence will be a strong indicator to them that you notice their poor behavior.

Step Three: If the first two steps do not work, then call a "timeout" and ask the group, "Don't we have a rule that says '*One person talks at a time*'?" This will really get their attention!

Question #10
"I'm going to start facilitating a new group next week. I met with the group's leader yesterday. How do I know the leader will *behave* himself during our meetings?"

Answer
Surely you discussed this with the leader during your initial meeting! But sometimes leaders have a short memory and resort back to the old behaviors of command and control during a meeting.

You as the facilitator must protect the rights of all participants in the meeting. If the leader starts to take control, try these interventions:

Intervention #1: After the leader makes a decisive remark, ask the group, "What do others in the group think...?"

Intervention #2: If the leader continues to dominate the process, just announce, "Let's take a break!" Then talk to the leader and remind the leader of your role (NOT theirs) to guide the process.

Question #11
"Yikes! Yesterday I got stuck and froze-up while facilitating. I couldn't think what to do next! What should I do if I cannot figure out what the next step is while in front of the group?"

Answer
Your best move would be to announce, "Let's take a break!"

During the break you will have time to regain your composure and think about your next step. You will also have time to refer to your reference material (like this text) or talk to knowledgeable people in the group about what to do.

If you cannot determine a next step during this break, then secure an *overnight recess* by suggesting to the group, "Can we quit for today and meet again tomorrow?" This will give you enought time to call me for advice.

Question #12

"Getting a group to concensus is so hard! Why can't we just vote to make a decision? It would be much faster!"

Answer

Sure, voting is always faster. But voting causes more damage to individuals in a group than the value of the time saved. Consider the following three points against voting:

First, voting forces most people to establish a position that is very, very hard to change *without looking foolish.*

Second, voting can heavily influences by *peer pressure.* Look at how people raise their hands only after looking around the room to see who's hands are up. That behavior cannot reflect true conviction about a decision!

Third, voting that uses a majority to decide the outcome *ignores the needs of the minority.* In other words, those individuals that "lose" in a vote... do youexpect them to immediately abandon their convictions? In most instances, the minority looks for revenge.

Non-binding "straw votes" are fine as indicators of where people are... but make it clear that the vote is just that, non-binding. *The best thing you can do is to talk, talk, talk until everyone feels comfortable with supporting the group's decision.*

Question #13

"There's one team member is very rude and antagonistic towards others in our group meeting. It is starting to affect attenance at our meetings. What should I do?"

Answer

You as the facilitator own the process. It is appropriate for you to take action in this situation to mitigate the threatening environment created by this person.

My recommendation is to extinguish this problem behavior immediately. A first step would be to ask the person, "Bob, I sense that you are very angry about something and I also feel that it is hurting our process. Can you help me understand your feelings?"

Warning: Don't start a debate in front of the group with this person. If the problem behavior does not stop, then call a time out and talk to the person privately. Tell him or her that their behavior is counterproductive to the process. *It is appropriate for you to ask him or her to leave the meeting.*

17 SELECTED RESOURCES

No one source is sufficient to learn facilitation skills.

There are many excellent sources of printed information regarding facilitation, group dynamics, consensus-building, and the processes surrounding group decision-making. A partial list is provided for the reader's use.

As a step beyond reading about it, there are several companies that specialize in classes and seminars on facilitation skills. Each provides interactive, facilitated-learning methods to increase the participants' understanding and retention of the material. Three of the best are shown.

And it follows, personal experience shows that the best way to become a good facilitator is to **do it**. There is no substitute for actually getting up in front of a group and being a facilitator! Do it!

Take every opportunity offered to you! Practice! Practice!

Good luck to each and everyone of you!

Printed Text

How to Make Meetings Work!, Michael Doyle & David Straus. Berkley Books, 1976. ISBN 0-425-13870-4. *Topics: What goes wrong at meetings, win/win solutions, being a good facilitator, planning your meeting, making meeting rooms work, tools for solving problems in groups, training yourself.*

How to Survive a Training Assignment, Steven K. Ellis. Addison-Wesley Publishing Company, 1988. ISBN 0-201-06647-5. *Topics: working with adult learners, instructional techniques, visual aids, effective presentations, evaluation & feedback.*

The Compleat Facilitator, Barry J. Roberts & Kevin Upton . Howick Associates, 1994. ISBN 0-9646972-0-3. *Topics: problem solving, dealing with people, meeting management, dealing with conflict, preventing people problems, implementation.*

Faultless Facilitation: A Resource Guide for Group and Team Leaders, Lois B. Hart. HRD Press, Inc. (telephone 800-822-2801), 1992. ISBN 0-97425-167-2. *Topics: understanding leadership and facilitation, getting off on the right foot, warming up the group, unspoken messages, clarifying and ranking problems, visual aids.*

Skill-Building for Self-Directed Team Members, Ann & Bob Harper. MW Corporation (telephone 914-528-0888), 1994. ISBN 1-880859-02-5. *Topics: team ground rules (with exercises), reaching consensus (with exercises), listening skills, group dynamics, managing conflict, role of facilitator.*

The Winning Trainer, Julius E. Eitington. Gulf Publishing Company, 1989. ISBN 0-87201-911-X. *Topics: problem identification, brainstorming, choosing alternatives, do's & don'ts, seating to facilitate participation, flipcharting, using silence.*

Flip Charts - How to Draw Them and How to Use Them, Richard C. Brandt. Pfeiffer & Company, 1986. ISBN 0-88390-031-9. *Topics: basics of using flip charts, markers, printing, color, balance & symmetry, transportation, storage.*

Body Language, Julius Fast. Pocket Books/ Simon & Schuster Inc., 1970. ISBN 0-671-67325-4. *Topics: what your posture says, movement & the message, postures & presentations.*

<u>Facilitation Skills for Team Leaders</u>, Donald Hackett & Charles L. Martin. Crisp Publications (telephone 415-323-6100), 1993. *Topics: encouraging participation, body language, essential tools, getting group agreement, what to do if the group gets stuck.*

<u>The Facilitator's Toolkit</u>, Lynn Kearny. Human Resources Development Press, Inc. (telephone 800-822-2801), 1995. ISBN 0-87425-268-7. *Topics: creative thinking with groups, six basic group needs, content & process, getting basic agreements.*

<u>Facilitation: Providing Opportunities for Learning</u>, Trevor Bentley. McGraw-Hill, 1994. ISBN 0-07-707684-2. *Topics: working with groups, intervention strategies, managing interaction.*

<u>Effective Meeting Skills</u>, Marion Haynes. Crisp Publications (telephone 415-323-6100), 1988. ISBN 0-931961-33-5. *Topics: handling difficult situations, managing conflict, providing feedback.*

<u>The Facilitators' Handbook</u>, John Heron. Nichols Publishing/GP Publishing, New York, 1989. ISBN 0-89397-355-6. *Topics: modes of facilitation, facilitator role, decision-making, interventions.*

Learning Programs

Here's a list of organizations offering classes in facilitation...

American Management Association
135 West 50th Street
New York, NY 10020
(212) 586-8100
The AMA has many, many courses (1, 2, 3, or 4-day) that are profession-
ally done and worth the cost of tuition and travel. They have learning
centers in Atlanta, Boston, Chicago, Kansas City, Washington, DC, San
Francisco, and New York, as well as special classes scheduled in other US
& Canadian cities. The AMA also offers self-paced and distance-learning.

Interaction Associates, Inc.
600 Townsend Street, Suite 550
San Francisco, CA 94103
(415) 241-8000
IA is a consulting firm specializing in real-life facilitation. They offer
courses in Facilitative Leadership, Mastering Meetings, and Facilitating
Change. They also offer a week-long "Facilitator Institute" that teaches
people how to use their "Interaction Method."

MW Corporation
3150 Lexington Avenue
Mohegan Lake, NY 10547
(914) 528-0888
Ann and Bob Harper creatively teach an entire series of classes directed at
the self-directed work teams, facilitators, train-the-trainer, active listen-
ing, team development, and customer service.

INDEX

K

KISS: 4-3

L

leader -
facilitator's relationship with: 8-1
initial meeting: 8-2
logistics, pre-meeting: 9-1

M

Management commitment: xi
mutual respect: xi

N

negative voting: 13-5
neutral facilitator: xiv, xv, 12-3

O

order form: front of book

P

paper method of brainstorming: 3-4
participation, promoting: 1-5
pledge, facilitator: xiii
points, first meeting: 12-7
positive: 1-5
possibilities: 3-1
process, owner: xvi

Q

questions -
frequently asked: 16-1 to 16-7
open-ended: 1-5

R

resources -
general: xi
selected: 17-1 to 17-4
risks: xi
role models: xi
room arrangement: 11-2
round robin method of brainstorming: 3-4

rules for group -
advanced: 12-5
basic: 12-4
rules, brainstorming: 3-2, 3-5

S

silence: 1-5, 3-3
stakeholders: 12-8
started, getting: 7-1
steps -
of facilitation process: xii, 12-6
of first meeting: 12-1
straw voting: 13-5
success -
general: xi
looks like: 12-7

T

task of group: 12-7
thoughts: 2-1
timing: 12-7
toolkit, facilitator's: 10-2
tools for consensus: 13-5
trust: xi

V

voting -
fist or five method: 13-6
negative: 13-5
straw: 13-5

W

welcome letter: 9-2
win-lose: 1-5
win-win: 1-5, 13-5
worksheet, pre-meeting: 8-3